Theology and the Disciplines of the Foreign Service

Theology and the Disciplines of the Foreign Service

The World's Potential to Contribute to the Church

THEODORE L. LEWIS

FOREWORD BY
STANLEY HAUERWAS

WIPF & STOCK · Eugene, Oregon

THEOLOGY AND THE DISCIPLINES OF THE FOREIGN SERVICE
The World's Potential to Contribute to the Church

Copyright © 2014 Theodore L. Lewis. All rights reserved. Except for brief quotations in critical publications or reviews, no part of this book may be reproduced in any manner without prior written permission from the publisher. Write: Permissions. Wipf and Stock Publishers, 199 W. 8th Ave., Suite 3, Eugene, OR 97401.

Wipf and Stock
An Imprint of Wipf and Stock Publishers
199 W. 8th Ave., Suite 3
Eugene, OR 97401

www.wipfandstock.com

ISBN 13: 978-1-4982-0603-7

Manufactured in the U.S.A.   12/16/2014

At the request of the Department of State, a disclaimer is herewith included:

The opinions and characterizations in this book are those of the author, and do not necessarily represent official positions of the United States Government.

In memory of my older son

Matthew Edward Lewis

On whom fell especially the cost of my discovery of
the links between theology and the Foreign Service

Contents

Foreword by Stanley Hauerwas | ix
Preface | xiii

Prologue | 1
1   Stepping onto the Road | 18
2   A Plethora of Potholes | 32
3   Seminary: Agony and Ecstasy | 43
4   A Highly Incongruous Parish | 61
5   Again in Vietnam | 70
6   Congo Embassy and Church | 81
7   Korea, Laos, and Washington Termination | 92
8   Properly into Theology | 110
9   Still Further into Theology | 124

Epilogue | 136
Annex: The Book Recast as Sermon | 165

Illustrations

Guard tower, rural Vietnam | 30
French Protestant Church, Saigon | 36
Bishop of Singapore's Saigon visitation | 80
Boga clergy and church | 90
Canon Apolo Kivebulaya | 91
Korean picnic | 96

Foreword

Ted Lewis is a modest man with a fierce intelligence. Because he is modest one can miss the fierceness of his intelligence. To describe Ted's intelligence as fierce is but a way of suggesting what an independent mind he has—in pursuit of the vision that has been given him. He is going to think what he thinks must be thought if one is to be faithful to the gospel, whether you agree with him or not. Moreover, he thinks what he thinks matters. Working basically alone, he is determined to think through what challenges face the church today in a manner that will help us all better know the road ahead. He pursues his vocation, moreover, outside any academic context but it is not to the academy he writes. Rather he writes for Christians who know something is wrong, and are open to the possibility, as well as the urgency, of setting it right.

One of the great benefits of writing is that other people read what you write, and sometimes they contact you to let you know they have read what you've written. That is how I met Ted Lewis. In *Theology and the Disciplines of the Foreign Service* he gives an account of his contacting me because of what he had read. He is the kind of reader that understands better than I what I've written. Ted and I have now known one another for over fifteen years and I long valued his visits with me in Durham. We have also stayed in touch through correspondence.

I was initially attracted to Ted's work because he brought me *To Restore the Church: Radical Redemption History to Now* (the composition of which makes up much of the story he tells in his present book). I read through the book and thought, "How remarkable! Here is an account of human history

Foreword

that Yoder could have written and yet he does not know Yoder at all!" Ted's account had come through reading scripture as a narration of the world in which we find ourselves. *To Restore the Church* is a book that most "smart" academics would not risk. There are too many judgments made in the book that an academic would have qualified so thoroughly that finally the book would have become uninteresting.

Ted, however, with that desire to get it right stormed ahead helping us see how the church's captivity to state formations has severely compromised our witness to the sovereignty of God. Ted's claim, for example, that the story of modern Germany may be seen as stemming from Luther's tragic failure to relate his theology of the cross to history is an extraordinary observation that I think is largely, though astonishingly, right. Moreover, Ted supports the observation by offering a remarkable account of modern Germany's history that climaxes tragically in the Holocaust. Anyone reading the chapter on Germany in *To Restore the Church* cannot help but recognize that this is a remarkable person.

Ted makes clear in *To Restore the Church* that it is in the church's powerlessness that its true power lies. But the freedom that powerlessness provides is only found if God is the God found in the calling of Israel and the cross and resurrection of Christ. Strong theological commitments are made throughout the book so that we may see the kind of work possible when those commitments are taken straight up. All of the virtues found in *To Restore the Church* are clearly on display in this book, *Theology and the Disciplines of the Foreign Service*.

Some may find it strange that I would commend this book. After all, Ted has been a faithful servant of the State Department—a service detailed in this memoir. But it is exactly because of the kind of servant Ted has been to the Foreign Service that makes his story so compelling.

Ted Lewis has led a remarkable life. Moreover, he tells the story of that life with such fascination and curiosity that this book is something of a page-turner. I cannot help but wonder: how do you put together this World War II soldier, who went to Haverford to be formed by the Quakers, only to complete his education at Harvard? The story becomes even more complex as he enters the Foreign Service and serves in Vietnam, the Congo, Pakistan, and Korea. And yet an already complex story becomes even more so when he is called to the priesthood and goes to seminary—only to discover profound tensions between his seminary education and what he takes to be the challenge of the gospel. It is an extraordinary story of an extraordinary life.

Foreword

Theology and the Disciplines of the Foreign Service is a book that is intellectually exciting precisely because Ted's commitment to telling the truth about his life. In order to display the coherence of his life, Ted draws on theological and philosophical insights that are at once simple and profound. But the heart of this book is a strong claim about how his training in the Foreign Service, a craft-like training, was the preparatory formation he needed to recognize how natural theology can be expressed within the revelation of God in Christ. He has read Barth and Brunner and he is able, through the telling of his life, to help us see how the famous Barth/Brunner exchange illumines the narrative character of his and our lives.

I confess I take some pride in thinking that my book *Hannah's Child* may influence the story he tells in *Theology and the Disciplines of the Foreign Service*. Ted's focus on craft knowledge as an indication of how one might think of natural theology, may have been partly learned by my account of bricklaying in *Hannah's Child*. The kind of craft he describes as integral to the Foreign Service seems very different from the craft of laying brick, but I think the reader will discover that the two are not as distant as they may seem. Of course, crucial to his account is the recognition that a natural theology determined by the craft analogy only works within a more determinative account of revelation.

The readers of this book will learn a great deal about what it means to serve in the Foreign Service of the United States of America. I know I have certainly learned to have great respect for those engaged in that discipline through the reading of this book. Ted Lewis has done what I think should be done by those influenced by so-called narrative theology, that is, he has not talked about narrative—he has shown how it works.

Ted Lewis is a modest man with a fierce intelligence. He thinks thoughts that challenge our conventions of thought. I hope this book will find the readers it so richly deserves because this remarkable man has given us a gift in the telling of his life.

Stanley M. Hauerwas
Gilbert T. Rowe Professor Emeritus of Divinity and Law
Duke Divinity School, Durham, North Carolina

Preface

I HAD A TWENTY-NINE-YEAR Foreign Service career, including postings in Vietnam, Pakistan, the Congo, Korea, and Laos. As it proceeded, I discovered many links between it and theology. The body of this book is the narrative of these discoveries. In its epilogue, I draw their implications for theology and the world. The book is meant to show not just what theology and the Foreign Service's disciplines are in themselves but also how they fit together, something I am reasonably sure has not been done before. The fact that they do fit together has implications of the most far-reaching, for theology and for the world. The Foreign Service provides a paradigm of the world's professions and occupations, in a word its crafts, to the disciplines of which theology gives new meaning. This meaning is that these disciplines have the potential to illuminate theology and in so doing to give it fresh vitality. Further, bringing theology and the world together in this fashion affords a resolution to a basic theological issue heretofore not fully resolved, namely how the two can and should relate to each other—the essential concern of natural theology. And in this resolution may be seen the possibility of a new instantiation of Pentecost, the church's Big Bang.

These are audaciousness claims, raising immediately the matter of my qualifications to make them. Do I have sufficient standing as a theologian? Can I really speak for the Foreign Service? Is there any reason to take seriously claims such as these by a previously unknown author? The full answers to these questions will be developed in the body of this book, but I can indicate them here.

Preface

As a theologian, by many standards I do fall short. I am not an academic and neither do I have a PhD. To be sure, I am a seminary graduate, but one does not really learn much about theology in seminary. I have been an Anglican priest for almost a half century, but that is no guarantee of theological knowledge either. My most notable qualification is the immense privilege of having been for long years under the tutelage of two of the world's best-known theologians, Alister McGrath of Oxford University and Stanley Hauerwas of the Duke Divinity School. Anything I have achieved is by dint of standing on their shoulders. I would add that a Foreign Service career such as mine prepares one well, even uniquely, for an understanding of theology.

My Foreign Service credentials might also be questioned, and I need to provide answers although they may be of limited intelligibility to those outside the foreign affairs community. Within the Department of State, which *de jure* has primary responsibility for the implementation of United States foreign policy, there are two main classes of employees: civil service, staffing mainly its Washington offices, and foreign service, mainly assigned to posts overseas. Within the latter class there is a further division: between those concerned with economic assistance under the associated US Agency for International Development and those directly under the State Department. Only in the latter does one qualify as a Foreign Service Officer (FSO). In my career of twenty-nine years I spent just seven as an FSO, preceded by three in the civil service and followed by nineteen in USAID. Yet I am undertaking to speak as an FSO, now retired. My justification is that my civil service was in the Bureau of Intelligence Research, closely attuned to reporting from overseas embassies; and in all but one of my overseas USAID postings I was a member of a joint embassy-USAID economic section, with my efficiency reports being written by an FSO. I wrote efficiency reports on one or two FSOs myself. Besides these things, my initial formation was as an FSO, and I have never really departed from it.

In some ways, though, my definitive qualification is my own career and the extent to which in this book I have conveyed its reality and its cost. For it is out of this career and the links with theology that I discovered in the course of it that the claims I am making have arisen. In the chapters forming the body of this book I have striven for total honesty, facing squarely my own shortcomings as well as the limitations imposed by the circumstances in which I found myself. For only through such honesty can my career sustain my claims. As for why I have waited until so late in life to make them, it is only now that I have arrived at the necessary comprehension to do so.

Preface

At several points my career and life took highly improbable turns, without any of which this book would not have come into being—a book embodying not only the meaning of my career but also the narrative coherence of my life. These turns in their improbability may be regarded as mere coincidence or else as providential, brought about by the Lord in the furtherance of his purposes. I should be clear that I see them as providential; indeed, the ability of the Lord to bring good out of the most adverse circumstances can be regarded as the book's subtext. But I have left the nature of these turns unspecified so that readers may come to their own conclusions.

I need also to say wherein my Anglicanism consists. I have had the title of resident theologian at All Saints' Church, Chevy Chase, Maryland, located in the Washington diocese of The Episcopal Church (TEC). Thus, formally, I am a priest of TEC. But my alignment is with those who have broken away from TEC to form a new province (Anglican Church in North America), seeing TEC as having departed from biblical obedience. Consistent with this, theologically I have come down on the side of Karl Barth, manifestly the greatest theologian of the twentieth century. For already by the early decades of the century Barth understood the surpassing worth of biblical obedience.

I have already alluded to the magnitude of my debt to McGrath and Hauerwas. Chapters 8 and 9 will describe it in detail. Without the trouble they have taken with me, busy as they are, not only would this book have been impossible, my formation in theology would have been only rudimentary. From my personal contact with McGrath's surpassing brilliance and vast energies during my years in Oxford, I was able to pick up something of what I lacked of these qualities. His expositions of historical theology in the 1980s and 1990s were formative for me. And his turn to natural theology in this century has provided the framework into which I could set my own concept of the relation between theology and the world, the underlying concern of natural theology. Coincidentally, or providentially, his excellent *Emil Brunner: A Reappraisal*, published in early 2014, arrived at just the right time to consolidate my account of the 1934 exchange between Brunner and Barth regarding natural theology. I have drawn substantially on this exchange in elaborating my own formulation of natural theology, which is not without bearing on the dividing issue in the church today.

As for Hauerwas, his distinctive and pervasively influential understandings of Christian narrative and community, of virtue and character, nicely complemented the grounding I received from McGrath. And not

Preface

only did he put me up to writing this book, in the wake of his doing so the way to convey the links between theology and the Foreign Service, which I had long felt to be critically important, came to me. It was by telling how in the course of my career I had come upon these links, without concern for what my telling might reflect on me or anybody else. In this I was probably inspired by his then-recent memoir *Hannah's Child,* in which he tells his own story, professional and personal, with his characteristic unflinching honesty. He is justly famous for his aphorisms; and when I protested that I was too obscure for anyone to heed what I wrote, he responded by coining one for me: The famous are too taken up with the story of what made them famous. My gratitude goes also to his wonderful assistant, Carole Baker.

On the Foreign Service side, my career was such that I have less by way of acknowledgements to make. I should not however fail to mention Roy Wehrle, Economic Counselor of Embassy and Associate Director for Program of the USAID Mission in Saigon in the latter 1960s, under whose direction I served. His grasp of the strategic issues, political as well as economic, in wartime Vietnam and his ability cogently to convey their urgency gave my thought and work a discipline which previously they did not have and which has carried over into my retirement. Also a significant influence, coming at the very beginning of my career, was FSO Norman Hannah, whose incisive political reporting from the American embassy in Bangkok, as I read it back in Washington, first awakened my critical faculties.

Notable among the several who encouraged me while I was writing was Richard Hays, probably America's best New Testament scholar and now Dean of the Duke Divinity School. The limitations of my biblical knowledge did not keep him from an interest in my work. I owe appreciation also to Margaret McConnell of Washington and Gillian Raven of Nairobi for their support. The encouragement of two others was of a special sort. Charlotte Jackson, who as a music major at the University of North Carolina was the first to read the early chapters of this book, confirmed that they were meaningful despite their having been excavated from the dimmer recesses of my memory. And Logan Gates, a student at the Oxford Center for Christian Apologetics, similarly was first to read and approve of my interpretation of the operation of the Holy Spirit at Pentecost, an interpretation on which my formulation of natural theology in fact depends. This book of course aims at those already formed in a profession or occupation—in my word in a craft. But since both Jackson and Gates are in their early twenties, their responses give hope that its appeal will extend to those not yet so formed.

Preface

My thanks are due to the Rev. Ed Kelaher, Rector of All Saints' Church, who on learning that Hauerwas had prompted me to write this book readily granted my request for a year's sabbatical, enabling me to make a proper start on it. My thanks are due no less to the people of All Saints', who in my decade-long association with them have been my effective family, providing me with a warm fellowship which otherwise I would have lacked. My one complaint is that they have been insufficiently critical.

May this book be accounted *non mihi sed soli Deo gloria*.

Germantown, Maryland
Pentecost, 2014

Liturgical citations are from the Episcopal Church's Book of Common Prayer, 1979. Biblical quotations are from the English Standard Version, 2011, or are my own translations.

Prologue

A year or two after my retirement from the Foreign Service I happened to pass through Paris, and I took the opportunity to look up a couple of former colleagues posted at the American Embassy there. They asked me, more than half seriously, "Is there life after the Foreign Service?" For those in the Foreign Service, operating as it does mostly overseas and mostly dealing with classified information, envisaging life on the outside can be difficult. I ventured a positive but hesitant answer to their question. With this book I am answering it with a resounding yes. Not only a life, but also a full life is possible, not as some totally new departure but in continuity with the Foreign Service. Thus those formed by its disciplines are greatly privileged. But all privileges entail responsibilities, and theirs entails one of prime importance. It is for the actualization of the potential inherent in their formation.

To be sure, the focus of this book is on the Foreign Service. But the potential to be found in its disciplines is bound to exist also in the disciplines of other professions and occupations, at least when practiced with the commitment that similarly as crafts they call forth. And of them the Foreign Service may be taken as the paradigm. Hence, we can speak of a potential granted to the world.

THE FOREGOING IS IMPLICIT in the title *Theology and the Disciplines of the Foreign Service*. The juxtaposition of the Foreign Service with theology may seem odd, almost as odd as the juxtaposition in the title of the 1974 best seller *Zen and the Art of Motorcycle Maintenance* (but this book is really about theology and the Foreign Service). Apart from academic theologians and members of the Foreign Service, few people would have a clear picture of either theology or the Foreign Service, and virtually no one of both. Indeed, in many ways they are polar opposites. But the link between them is real; moreover, it has implications of cardinal importance for the church and for the world, no less than for retirees like me. To the church, the link offers the vitality to carry out its still unfulfilled mission, the vitality of a new Pentecost (to use a still-to-be-explained Christian term). To the world, it offers a meaning it could not otherwise have through its participation in this vitality. And to my fellow retirees, it offers challenges even more compelling than those they encountered in their active service.

To convey the reality of the link I must tell the story of my discovery of it over the course of my twenty-nine-year career in the Foreign Service which formed me. I must also tell the story of my concurrent and subsequent ordained ministry. By doing so I will show that the link is not a mere intellectual abstraction or some academic construct but has its basis in very concrete realities—personal and of recent history. My career, extending from 1951 to 1984, was framed by the Cold War, the then pervasive contest with the Soviet Union. After telling how I got the idea of a Foreign Service career and then acted upon it, I will describe my postings successively in Vietnam, Australia, Pakistan, Vietnam (again), the Congo, Korea, and Laos, with the exception of Australia all marked by conflict if not by actual war, and finally in Washington—with a break for seminary and a parish ministry along the way. I will follow this with my post-retirement acquisition of theological knowledge beyond what I learned in seminary, beginning in Oxford and continuing back in America. In an Epilogue, I will set out the significance of my account for the church, for the world, and for my fellow retirees—how by virtue of the disciplines of Foreign Service and other crafts the way to a major theological advance now lies open.

Most Foreign Service memoirs seem intent on magnifying the authors' career achievements and/or vindicating their policy judgments that failed to be accepted at the time. This is not a memoir of that sort. Instead, where the Foreign Service is concerned, it will tell of a career which, by the usual standards, was a failure. It will be as honest as I can make it, which is necessary if it is to convey my career's relevance to theology. It will tell also how through my discovery of this relevance my ignominy was transformed, so as to call for assessment by a quite other standard. To be sure, my discovery came at a cost. But in view of what was at stake, I could not have refused it in conscience.

Prologue

The ancient Greek myth of Prometheus may have some relevance here. It was Prometheus who stole fire from the gods and gave it to mortals, putting them in possession of a power they had not had before. Perhaps I may be seen as appropriating the fire to be derived from the Foreign Service for the general benefit. The gods penalized Prometheus for his audacity, condemning him to have an eagle perpetually eat his liver. Presumably he had expected to get away with what he did and so underwent this punishment unwillingly. From this standpoint he may be seen as symbolizing the overreaching of human limitations and the consequences of so doing, as many have seen him. But if he knew what he would be obliged to suffer and accepted it for the sake of humanity, his story takes on a different complexion. There was, in fact, a man who accepted suffering and death in order to bring a surpassing gift to humanity. This was not just in myth but also in history, moreover at a pivotal point. My hope is that the cost I incurred may somehow be taken up in the one borne by him, the Christian Lord.

My story will not be meaningful, however, unless the Foreign Service can be made intelligible to theologians and theology intelligible to Foreign Service people—and both to the far larger number with little knowledge of either. Volumes have been written about both, especially about theology. My undertaking will be modest, intended to cover only those features of both which are needed for an understanding of their relationship. Out of solidarity with my former Foreign Service colleagues, I will be at special pains to make theology intelligible to them. I will begin with an explication of the Foreign Service as it is perhaps easier to convey. This will be the Foreign Service that I knew, if not always and everywhere then at its limits. I will write about it in the present tense. There have been changes since then, to be sure, but underlying them there must be a basic continuity.

The Foreign Service

The external features of the Foreign Service are evident enough. It is a component of the Department of State, to which is assigned responsibility for the foreign relations and interests of the United States. It staffs mainly American embassies, consulates, and missions around the world, but its members are given Washington assignments as well. Along with constituting the point of contact with foreign governments, it performs a variety of functions, among them consular, administrative, commercial, cultural, and public informational. But the core function is to gather, analyse, and report on political and economic information by officers in overseas posts—to serve as bases for policy decisions back in Washington.

It should be added that the Foreign Service is intended to be instrumental in implementing policy handed down by policy-makers rather than formulating or critiquing it. It avows loyalty to whatever administration is in office, which is seen as a limitation from some standpoints. Still, the Foreign Service is necessarily involved in policy through the supplying of the information and analyses on which policy is based. This does not mean that its members may not have their own divergent opinions. Indeed, they often do, given that their overseas reporting calls for development of critical faculties to a high degree. Often they can argue for these opinions vigorously in-house, but there is no assurance that their dissent will be heeded; additionally, if their opposition goes to the point of conscience, their only recourse is to resign.

The Service's internal features are less accessible. By virtue of the time they spend overseas, its members, while their exposure to foreigners is substantial, are limited in their contacts with other Americans. Further, the data they deal with are mostly classified and cannot be discussed with outsiders. At the same time, they lack the conveniences, familiar surroundings, and physical protections generally available in America. Thus for those without direct experience of them, its internal features may not be fully understandable. Still, I would be surprised if these features do not have counterparts in other organizations and institutions. To the extent that I am able to convey them to outsiders, these counterparts should become recognizable.

To begin with, the Foreign Service is culturally not quite of America; in fact, it is something of a subculture. It partakes of the prevailing American individualism but it is corporate to a greater extent than perhaps other American civilian organizations. This is evident largely through its decidedly hierarchical structure. It has a nine-grade rank ladder, rising from entry level, already on the basis of competitive examination, to Career Ambassador. In inter- and intra-office relations, rank order is closely observed. The effects of hierarchy are not entirely negative, however. One knows where one stands and what one is expected to do, as also in hierarchical societies of the past. There is reciprocity of obligation—of superiors to subordinates as well as of subordinates to superiors. An effect of this is that in the Foreign Service one is kept fully informed of what is going on.

A case in point is the staff meetings of the Foreign Service. The meetings will be chaired by one's superior, whether ambassador or section chief

Prologue

or office director, who will be expecting from all present accounts of what they have been doing—and they better be prepared to give succinct and cogent ones. In this way, everyone knows what everyone else is involved in. But no less significantly, the meeting will begin with an account from the superior of what has been going on at the higher levels of the embassy or bureau, thus providing a framework for the others to fit into.

The Foreign Service is highly disciplined, in ways reminiscent of ancient Rome or perhaps the pre-World War II German general staff. Tolerance for error is nearly zero. If you slip up, you can expect withering scorn from your supervisor. Members whose performance does not meet expectations are liable to being transferred or even separated from the Service. The Romans' discipline was evident in their devotion of whatever resources were necessary to attain their objectives, whether establishment of their hegemony in the Italian peninsula or defeat of Carthage in the contest for control of the Mediterranean. A reflection of this can be seen in modern-day Britain dating from its Roman occupation. Any road in Britain that goes straight for a considerable distance is almost certainly an old Roman road.

The Foreign Service approaches objectives in a similar way. It demands total commitment on the part of its members, not just during office hours but at all times. However difficult the assignment you are given, you accomplish it; however tight your deadline, you meet it. And woe betides you if any details in your reports turn out to be inaccurate, whether or not they affect your conclusions. Nor is this attention to detail merely arbitrary, a manifestation of perfectionism. The Service's experience over the decades has shown that you can never be sure which details will turn out to be significant. Finally, you are expected not to have regard for danger to yourself or hardship for your family. The dangers to be encountered are not negligible; between the Vietnam War and the wars in Iraq and Afghanistan, the Foreign Service had a higher fatality rate in line of duty than the military. The lengthy, and lengthening, memorial plaques in the State Department's main entrance attest to this.

In part, this discipline is instilled by the intense competition that the promotion system fosters; herein it partakes of American individualism. Promotion is on the basis of annual efficiency reports written by one's supervisor and submitted to promotion panels back in Washington, which then rank all officers in a particular grade against each other. The rewards of promotion are great, opening the way to wider possibilities and responsibilities while also conferring prestige: official rank largely determines personal worth. On the other hand, failure to achieve promotion at a sufficiently rapid rate leads to "selection out," that is, separation from the Service. The system has little use for those who are seen as not productive or as having ceased to be. Selection out is a serious matter, especially if the Foreign Service is considered a lifetime career, as it was in my day. I knew of two suicides which "selection out" occasioned. The writing of efficiency reports thus confers on supervisors a quasi life-and-death power. Insofar as individual advancement is sought through the furtherance of overall objectives and not through ingratiation with one's supervisor, it is consistent with the Service's generally corporate nature. When this is not the case, however, it introduces an element of incoherence. Of course, exposure to the rigors of the promotion system renders acute one's sense of vulnerability; as an experience shared with colleagues, though, it constitutes an element of fellowship with them.

This overtly competitive promotion system explains only part of the Foreign Service's discipline. Probably the larger part is attributable to the deep commitment to their duties found among its members. And this as also other internal features is to be understood in terms of a critical turn in the history of the State Department, and thus of the Foreign Service. The State Department's history is long, going back to 1789 and to Thomas Jefferson as the first Secretary of State. But only in the wake of World War II did the Foreign Service assume its present character. For then the United States, which had been a lesser player on the world stage, abruptly emerged as a superpower, moreover one locked in an apparent struggle for survival with the Soviet Union, somewhat as Rome and Carthage had been in the ancient Mediterranean world. This was a serious business, subjecting the Foreign Service to extreme new demands in a very short time. It is not surprising that it should respond in the drastic ways just cited, substituting them for the niceties of protocol prevailing in a previously small and élite corps (which seems nevertheless to have passed on its determinedly secular cast).

This historical turn explains more than these features. It casts light also on why, despite the hazards to which it subjects its members, the Foreign Service maintains exceptionally high levels of performance. Above all it accounts for the thoroughgoing commitment with which its members respond. For it confers on them a responsibility for carrying out a vital mission, bearing on the lives of millions. This not only advances the interests of the United States but also the welfare and peace of the world. The welfare and peace of the world can be seen as synergistic with the interests of the

United States. Moreover, responsibility is borne not individually but jointly, by teams the members of which rely implicitly on each other to perform the functions assigned to them. The work of the Foreign Service is nothing if not teamwork; even at the highest levels I doubt that decisions are taken solo. Working together with one's fellows to achieve an end held in common to be good was for Aristotle the condition for *eudaimonia,* the state of happy wellbeing.

To be sure, some have contended, not without reason, that there is an illusionary element in this synergism, that the welfare and peace in question are as defined by the United States but often not by others. But even they must concede that when the Foreign Service slips up, the consequences can be disastrous. And the closer one gets to where decisions are finally made, the more one is impressed with the fragility of the whole international system. No less than Bismarck, the nineteenth century "Iron Chancellor" who brought about Germany's reunification, in speaking of the possibility of a European war being set off "by some damn fool thing in the Balkans" (as in fact it was), recognized this fragility. The avoidance of slip-ups—which confers a sense not of power but of responsibility—along with the promotion of general welfare and peace can qualify as an end commonly held to be good.

Of course, commitment by itself is not sufficient. It requires a concomitant development of professional capabilities, in the case of the Foreign Service particularly analytical and critical skills. It requires also initiation into the Service's traditions. As products of the situations confronting it in the past together with the modes in which these have been responded to, they are more than just the templates ordering its internal and external functioning. They give it its distinctive character, by which it is differentiated from a mere machine, much as personality differentiates an individual from a robot. Neither of these two requirements can be met overnight. Only through long apprenticeship to those already versed in them, coupled with experience of applying them to the unyielding realities of foreign relations, can this be accomplished.

Commitment will be insufficient also unless conjoined with virtues such as courage, fairness, and discernment. To some extent these must be already present in members, deriving from the educations and experiences that they bring with them. But commitment can also draw them forth. I will cite two particularly meaningful experiences in my own career. One was of being called on to do things I did not think I could do or even thought that

I could not, and discovering that I could do them after all. The other was of being relied on absolutely by my colleagues to perform my part in a critical task assigned to us while I similarly relied on them, and of having our mutual expectations fulfilled. Altogether the Foreign Service is conducive to the development of skills and talents rather like the internal goods that Aristotle saw as generated by practices promoting the welfare of ancient Athens.

Thus the structures and disciplines of the Foreign Service provide a framework within which its members' talents are called forth and can develop. But like all human institutions, it is subject to corruption, as through putting its institutional interests above the wider purposes it is called to serve and through the personal interest of its bureaucrats in maintaining their standing. And as this happens it stifles the very talents that it has called forth. Even apart from this, these talents or internal goods—which figure prominently in our later discussion—are likely to develop a kind of surplus, beyond the point where they are fully applicable within the Foreign Service. Their applicability necessarily ceases on the member's retirement. So the Foreign Service can be only provisional in providing their final end or goal. A still greater arena will be required for their complete realization. The identification of the one to which they may thus be seen as pointing, their *telos* in Christian as well as Aristotelian terms, is the purpose of this book. It will be seen as theology.

Theology

In terms accessible to Foreign Service members and other non-theologians, what is theology? I am aware that many would regard theology with suspicion, even more that they would the Foreign Service, and I will answer out of an awareness of that as well as of the unfamiliarity of many with it. Etymologically the term is straightforward. It comes from the Greek words *Theos*, meaning God, and *logos*, meaning reasoning in this case. Accordingly, theology is reasoning about God, an unexceptionable concept given God's existence. But it is not some generic theology that we are talking about here. On the contrary, it is one that would seem quite alien from a Foreign Service standpoint, and would shock many churchgoers as well. The paradox is that solely on this basis can a valid link with the Foreign Service be made. Other theologies, distinguishing less radically between God and the world, may seem more promising, but their promise cannot be sustained. If the link can be made validly with a Foreign Service that epitomizes secularity, then likely the link can be made also with other secular professions and occupations.

The radicalness of this theology becomes apparent as we pursue our inquiry. For we must next ask, on what basis are we to reason about God? Clearly it must be on the basis of knowledge of God. But what is this knowledge and where do we get it? This time, it is the knowledge that God discloses about himself. But we are not yet through with our outrageous assertions. As for wherein God reveals himself, it is in his word as set forth in Scripture, meaning the Old and New Testaments of the Christian Bible. To this, even believers may object that God gives signs of himself also in nature, in philosophical speculations, and in our inner consciousness as parts of his creation. In this, they are not entirely wrong. But they need to bear in mind that only in the light cast on them by Scripture can these signs be rightly discerned. And Scripture's light is itself the work of the Holy Spirit.

This forgoing is necessarily abstract apart from some account of the biblical contents. A considerable one will be given later on in this book, particularly in chapter 3. But in view of prevailing biblical unfamiliarity, it would be well to give some idea of them now. For the most part the Bible consists of historical narrative, coupled with reflections on that narrative. The narrative centers on the events by which God has saved his people, the nation of Israel and then the church. Three of them may be cited as crucial. The first is his deliverance of the Israelites from their slavery in Egypt. The second is his enabling through the prophets of the perseverance of Israel's faith, despite the destruction of the nation and the exile of the people by the Assyrians and Babylonians. The third is the life, death, and resurrection of Jesus as his incarnate Son, through which the world is redeemed.

It is in the light of the third that a common element can be seen in all three. This is the acceptance of human powerlessness as opening the way for the power manifested in God's saving acts to enter in. Moses in the Exodus, Israel's decisive moment, exemplifies this acceptance. When the Israelites whom he is leading out of Egypt are trapped by Pharaoh's pursuing army at the sea, they despair. But Moses, instead of despairing, calls on them to stand fast and await God's deliverance. God then accomplishes it by allowing the Israelites to pass through the sea. The prophets, when confronted by the catastrophe of destruction and exile impending over the nation, face it squarely instead of diverting their gaze from it as most did. In doing so, they are empowered to see in it not God's forsaking of his people but instead their unfaithfulness to him. Divine power entering in the wake of acceptance of human powerlessness is manifested most directly in Jesus' obedience even to death on the cross. From his death ensued his resurrection, and with it the deliverance of humanity from the error into which it had fallen and from which it was unable to extricate itself. As for the nature of this error, it was to affirm rather than deny human power, to suppose that humans could take their lives into their own hands independent of any power above them. This, of course, is what Adam and Eve are portrayed as doing when they ate the fruit giving them their own knowledge of good and evil. Traditionally it is referred to as "the Fall."

A further point: The deliverance wrought by Jesus' self-offering on the cross could not be effective so long as knowledge of it was confined to his own disciples. It had to become known also in the world around them. This was brought about through the Pentecost event. In it the disciples, gathered in Jerusalem fifty days after Jesus' resurrection, were impelled to proclaim publicly what God had accomplished in Jesus, that is to say, the good news, the literal meaning of the word "gospel." As they proclaimed the good news, the bystanders, who had come to Jerusalem from many nations, heard it as in their own native languages, meaning that in the light of it their own experiences and concepts became meaningful in a way they had not been before. And they believe it. Ceasing to be mere bystanders, they constitute themselves as the church and assume its functions. This signifies the way in which the peoples to whom the church subsequently carried the gospel received it. Through their reception of it, through their recognition that it imparted new meaning to their lives, fresh insights and energies became available to the church, contributing to its rapid spread in the ancient Roman world.

I have been making many assertions, all of them unsupported. The question arises of with reference to what they are to be authenticated. The answer here is the greatest outrage of all. There is no such reference; they are self-authenticating. There is no option other than to take them as the point of departure for all other knowledge, to accept the God of Israel and of Jesus Christ as the measure of all things. To set up something else—for example, nature or reason—as the measure of God is to make that something else into God, and so self-authenticating in turn.

Actually, these assertions are not alone in their outrageousness. Take, for example, Einstein's theory of relativity, wherein space and time, which for us are fixed quantities, are held to be relative or elastic; and quantum mechanics with its weird juxtapositions of energy and matter similarly partake of this quality. These approaches afford the best fit for the physical phenomena to which they relate. The same goes for theology. What at first seems impossible often turns out to be profoundly true—as with the world's potential to contribute to the church.

But even when we have taken this last most outrageous step, we do not find that all our questions have been resolved. If anything they have been enhanced. In the foreground is the one concerning the acceptance of our human powerlessness. The Foreign Service is certainly not into this. It is deeply involved in wielding the power—political, economic, and military—of the world's most powerful nation. How then can it have anything to do with an approach in which worldly power is superseded? A full answer must await the account of my career, which is the body of this book. But even here we may note that the discrepancy is not total. For we have observed that in the Foreign Service the closer one comes to policy decision making, the more one is struck with the fragility of the whole international system, with its liability to collapse from the breakdown of any of its constituents. Such an awareness of the limits of worldly power may be seen as converging with the acceptance of powerlessness posited above.

This is by no means the end of the questions now arising. At least two basic ones remain to be tackled: First, if Scripture is as compelling as it has been made out to be—if as in the sixteenth century formulation, "Holy Scripture containeth all things necessary for salvation"—can theology have any function beyond pointing to Scripture? Cannot Scripture be left to speak for itself? Secondly, is there something that we, as denizens of the work-a-day world, Foreign Service or other, are called to do in connection with theology? Are we to be mere bystanders or does a substantive role in fact now fall to us?

Indeed, theology has a further task, the one to which so many theologians have devoted themselves down through the centuries. It stems from the largely narrative nature of Scripture. Scripture, as the story of God's acts by which he has saved his people, is highly dramatic as noted in the above account of it. But it is not just for entertainment. If a story is a good one, it has implications, and Scripture has the most of all. However, whatever is implicit needs to be made explicit if it is to be actualized. A start on this was made already in the New Testament, particularly in the letters of St. Paul to the churches he established on his journeys in Asia Minor and in Greece. But by no means did these letters answer all the questions to which the Scriptures gave rise. To mention a few of them, the New Testament speaks of Jesus as God's Son, but in what way is he God's Son? With regard to Jesus himself, is he human or divine? Those who followed him after his resurrection were conscious of the Spirit, God's and his, working in them, but where does the Spirit fit in? They were keenly aware that Jesus, by sacrificing himself on the cross, had redeemed them from sin and death; this awareness had led them to become his followers. Further, they knew that they ought to live righteous lives. But did they still have to merit what he had done for them, in effect earn their salvation? Finally, although the pagan world around them was permeated with idol-worship and other practices unacceptable to Christians, its philosophy and literature had clearly positive aspects. Was it permissible for them to draw on these aspects in the elaboration of their faith, or did they have to shun their edifying along with their repugnant aspects?

These questions were not a matter of idle speculation; instead they were critical to the reality of the redemption that Jesus' followers had experienced. In order to be assured that it was real objectively and not merely subjectively, they needed answers: How could they relate to the Father, the Son, and both to the Spirit? How did the human and the divine natures within Jesus rank in relation to each other? What was the connection between their redemption by Jesus and their own efforts to be righteous? How should they regard the pagan world around them?

As we have seen, these questions arose directly from the situation in which Jesus' early followers found themselves. But they were given additional force by the concepts of Greek philosophy prevalent in the world into which Christianity emerged. People accustomed to thinking in terms of them wanted answers expressed in these terms. In this of course there was a danger: casting them in philosophical terms could lead to distortions, and to some extent it did. At the same time it served to bring out dimensions of the answers otherwise not apparent.

Providing answers, the task of theology, was thus of critical importance. It was also critical that these answers be the right ones, namely in accordance with revelation. For if instead they had their source in the values of the world, they would bring its values with them into the gospel, thereby undercutting its distinctiveness and thus its power. Answers of the latter sort were in fact put forward; for the world, the values of which the gospel calls into question, constantly attempts to domesticate it and so avert its judgment. Identifying these worldly answers was also the task of theology. It was anything but easy. For one thing, some such proposed answers were promoted with a vehemence that threatened to split the church. This was particularly true of Arianism, a doctrine that held that the Christ was not fully divine but instead a part, albeit the highest, of the created order. For another, in denying the truth of these answers, it was necessary to set out with precision what was to be affirmed in their place. And then the assent of the church to both the denials and the affirmations needed to be obtained.

Assenting to them was the function particularly of church councils, which became possible in the fourth and fifth centuries AD, when the church was no longer under persecution but instead received a measure of official support. The Council of Nicea meeting in 325 rejected the Arian attribution of Christ to the created order, asserting instead that he and God were of the same being, or *homoousios*—a Greek rather than a biblical term. And together with the Spirit whom the early Christians had experienced in their lives, they constituted the Trinity: one God in three Persons. An important ground for asserting the divinity of Christ was that only as divine could he have effected humanity's redemption. This, however, left open the question of how he could have effected it without also himself having participated in the human condition, or without having become "one of us." In response this question, the Council of Chalcedon meeting in 451 affirmed that he was both fully divine and fully human. As for how this could be, the Council wisely chose not to elaborate but instead to refer to Scripture for the explanation.

The answers given by these Councils were of course only bare statements, leaving many details as well the answers to other questions still to be provided. Individual theologians concerned themselves with providing them. Some did so even before the Council of Nicea, among whom Clement of Alexandria, Origen, and Tertullian were notable. In the period between Nicea and Chalcedon, perhaps in the whole history of Christian theology, the outstanding figure was Augustine. While basing himself on Scripture he drew also from Greek philosophy, specifically its Platonic stream. On these bases, he undertook to elaborate the concept of the Trinity as set forth at Nicea. In his controversy with Pelagius—who held that salvation could be earned by one's own efforts—he prevailed, maintaining that it could come only through God's grace. Particularly notable was his *City of God,* his extensive account of the relation of the Christian faith to the world around it, of the heavenly city to the earthly, how they differed even in their coexistence and therefore were not to be confused with each other. His drawing on Greek philosophy contributed to his insights, to be sure. But through its regularizing tendencies it may also have conditioned him to acceptance of the major role of the state in the church initiated by the Emperor Constantine and continuing for the most part thereafter.

In the theology of the Middle Ages, a similarly commanding role was played by Thomas Aquinas. Where Augustine had drawn on Platonism, or neo-Platonism, Aquinas drew on Aristotle, newly rediscovered in his time. In fact his enterprise consisted largely of showing how the Christian message, while remaining intact, could be expressed in Aristotelian terms. His was a towering achievement, resolving many questions which had remained unanswered: hence his title of Doctor of the Church. But in looking to natural law, accessible through human reason, as well as to divine revelation as a source of truth, he detracted somewhat from the primacy of Scripture. This perhaps opened the way to the reliance on tradition as well as Scripture still to be found in Roman Catholicism. Tradition, too, can be viewed as to some extent a human construct. Human construction implies a degree of human competence such as would be employed in earning salvation by one's own efforts—despite Augustine's refutation of this possibility.

The next notable stage in theological development was the Reformation, inaugurated by Luther and systematized and institutionalized by Calvin. In large part, it was a reaction to what was seen as deviation of the church from its basis in Scripture and as undue reliance not just on tradition but also on human authority. Although formally such reliance was never allowed, at the popular level a belief took hold that salvation could be earned by righteous deeds, by works.

Luther's doctrine of justification by faith gave the Reformation its distinctive form. He arrived at it through finding that his works of piety could never give him assurance of salvation, no matter how hard he tried. His only recourse then was to trust not in them, not in his own righteousness, but wholly in God's mercy. And having done so, he found God's mercy to be abundantly forthcoming. In the concept of justification by faith is to be seen perhaps the closest accord of all with the theme we discerned in biblical redemption history, namely that power lies ultimately in acceptance of our own powerlessness. In fact, this might be transposed as follows: justification lies ultimately in acceptance of our own unrighteousness. Essential to this doctrine is the surrender of all claims to the earning of salvation by our own efforts, the recognition that only God is able to effect this. Further, he can be trusted to do so. Indeed, he has already done in Jesus Christ. Trusting wholly in God led Luther to rely on God's revelation of himself in Scripture rather than on any human authority. This meant a break with the

Prologue

established ecclesiastical hierarchy and the doctrines developed in support of it, with the papacy and its associated dogmas. Thus the church in the West was divided into its Protestant and Catholic wings.

Accordingly, in the Protestant churches of the modern period, Scripture no longer had to contend with ecclesiastical tradition as a source of truth. It did not remain without a rival, however. Especially in the wake of the Enlightenment—with its feature of a universally accessible and valid reason—other sources, notably nature and philosophical concepts, began to be placed alongside it and over it. Human nature itself was increasingly seen as the point of departure for knowledge of God, with the limitations imposed by its finitude and sinfulness being relegated to the background. The process continued largely unchecked until the outbreak of World War I, the devastation of which cast into stark relief the inadequacy of the presuppositions, those of theological liberalism as it is termed, on which it was based.

The prime articulator of their inadequacy was Karl Barth, a Swiss theologian who from 1921 to 1935 taught and wrote in Germany. He saw them as having left the way open for not only the imperialism out of which World War I came but also the Nazism that overtook Germany in the 1930s. From opposing them, as he did initially in his bombshell account of St. Paul's Letter to the Romans, he went on to construct, in his fourteen-volume *Church Dogmatics,* a comprehensive replacement for them. Barth understood the need not just to oppose the liberalism they derived from, but also to provide a thoroughgoing alternative to it, based on rock rather than shifting sand. The outrageous assertions about the sufficient and self-authenticating nature of revelation with which this section began are in fact taken from him.

However, in the intensity of his reaction against theological liberalism he was led to disallow any contribution to knowledge of God from sources outside of revelation. He devoted a long section of his *Church Dogmatics* to refuting natural theology, as the relating of knowledge of God from "natural" sources to that from revelation is termed. He maintained that it was misleading, unwarranted despite apparent support in Scripture, and a principal instrument for domesticating the gospel so as to remove its threat to the human illusion of being in control. And this poses the starkest of dilemmas for our enterprise. On the one hand, we are basing it on his "outrageous" fundamental principles. On the other, we are aiming to make manifest the light that the Foreign Service, along with other secular professions and occupations, can and should cast on theology. These are part of the "natural" to which Barth objected so strenuously. Therefore, unless we can find a way out of this dilemma, unless we can show that our enterprise is consistent with his principles, it falls to the ground. Finding this way will be our concern in this book's Epilogue.

It is now that we come to the second of the two questions cited above as still to be dealt with, even after our discussion of theology had brought us to the sufficiency of Scripture. This question was whether as denizens of the work-a-day world we had a theological role to play other than as bystanders. The answer is that we do have a role, and it is to show that our enterprise is in fact consistent with Barthian principles; instead of a massive roadblock, these principles are our foremost asset. If we can show this, not only will we have made an important contribution to natural theology. We will also have opened a critical part of the way to the new Pentecost spoken of at the start of this Prologue. Out of it could come not only an infusion of vitality into the church but also the clarification of the church's message, now largely obscured. Our answer to this question also will be given systematic exposition in the Epilogue. First, though, the groundwork needs to be laid in the form of the account of my discovery of links between theology and the Foreign Service. What remains for this Prologue is to tell the extraordinary story of how this book came into being.

As a retired Foreign Service Officer and a member of the American Foreign Service Association, I receive the Association's monthly publication, *The Foreign Service Journal*. In the summer of 2011, it devoted an issue to the State Department's dissent channel. The channel was instituted to circumvent the situation in which subordinates are blocked by their ambassador or other superior from reporting what they perceived to be matters of urgency. (It must be acknowledged that such blockages have taken place; some ambassadors and other superiors are strongly averse to bad news.) To this end, it provides for dissents to go directly to the Secretary of State or at least his or her associates. The *Journal* issue put me in mind of the time I availed myself of the dissent channel. This was back in 1977 when, despite the end of the Vietnam War, the US was intent on keeping the new Vietnamese government at arms length. Citing my own official involvement with Vietnam over a twenty-seven-year period, including three years in-country, I argued that in twenty years or so we were bound to have normal relations with Vietnam anyway, as we had come to have with China, and

PROLOGUE

that it would be in the US interest to move toward them now. In the case of China, our waiting to establish relations until twenty years after the communist take-over could be seen as allowing the Korean War and other bad things to take place. My dissent had no perceptible policy effect, but I had the satisfaction of seeing diplomatic relations with Vietnam established in 1995, exactly twenty years after the Vietnam War ended.

Having been put in mind of this episode, I dashed off a letter about it to the journal's editor, not thinking much about it. To my surprise, it was published. I decided to send a copy to my theological mentor Professor Stanley Hauerwas at the Duke Divinity School, not supposing he would pay much attention either. He did, though, and when I visited him a couple of months later, on its basis he urged me to write about the Foreign Service and its theological links. I had, in fact, long thought that I ought to do this and had made a couple of attempts at it, without finding any adequate way to proceed. But in the wake of Hauerwas' urging, one came to me: it was to tell the story of my discovery of these links in the course of my Foreign Service career. This I will now do.

1

Stepping onto the Road

THE SEED WAS PLANTED at Camp Blanding, a sprawling infantry training camp in north-central Florida, in the latter stages of World War II. The tree that grew from it was a career in the Foreign Service, but the fruit that the tree bore, against nature and all expectation, was an absorption into theology. The way to this outcome was long and fraught with difficulties and dangers. It cost me dearly. But its improbable twists and turns brought me to a treasure that I ought not to keep to myself. At the same time, it showed how historical events—the history of the world, the history of our own lives—can lead us where we would not have thought to go but where we nevertheless ought to be.

The seed was planted there in April of 1945, and the weather was already hot. Along with a thousand or so of my fellow trainees, I was lined up in formation on the camp's vast parade ground. We had been assembled for the reading a proclamation concerning the death of President Roosevelt a week previously and the consequent succession of President Truman. As I listened I was impressed as I had not been before—I was still only eighteen—with the magnitude of the part Roosevelt had played in the world, with the responsibility that he had borne for people's lives not only in the nation but throughout the world. My childhood had been marked by a sense of isolation, of a lack of connection with much of anything beyond my school and my own family. This was due partly to my parents being rather isolated, but no less to the atmosphere prevailing in the 1930s of my childhood. With the nation in the grip of the Great Depression there seemed to be little that one could do to affect one's circumstances. In the wider world, the United States—being virtually unarmed at that time (incredible as this now seems)—had little with which to oppose the looming totalitarianism in Europe and Asia. Thus it was that in the moment of hearing the proclamation the desire came to me for some measure of Roosevelt's connection with larger affairs, as the remedy for my isolation and my powerlessness. As for how to attain to it, I was much too diffident to enter into the rough and tumble of domestic politics. I thought foreign relations, carried on with more order and less public exposure, would be open to me. I decided that a Foreign Service career would be what I aimed for once I got out of the army.

Infantry training during World War II, fought in both Europe and the Pacific, was arduous. It involved learning to shoot rifles, machine guns, mortars, and other weapons through long hours on the firing ranges. It involved conditioning through lengthy hikes and bivouacs. In the barracks there was an utter lack of privacy even for bodily functions, this I suppose so as to break down our civilian individuality. Our frequent sessions of close-order drill, the execution of precise marching manoeuvres in unison, utilized by the military immemorially to instil instant unreflecting obedience, also served this purpose. Sometimes we got weekend passes and so could visit nearby cities like St. Augustine and Jacksonville. Otherwise, we were under military discipline, constrained to follow the sergeant's orders, salute all officers, keep our boots shined, and get the blankets on our bunks so tight that a quarter would bounce off them. In these respects, we were a far cry from Willie and Joe, the slouching unshaven GIs of Bill Maudlin's mordant wartime cartoons. But we were not left without reminders of the realities of war. For example, we were exhorted when we came under fire from hedgerows ahead of us to aim our return fire at their base. This was because following the D-Day landing in Normandy, where series of hedgerows characterized the countryside, German soldiers had concealed themselves behind them. As they tried to advance, the Americans had aimed higher up, leaving them largely unscathed.

The composition of my training company was significant. At that stage of the war the armed services were scraping the bottom of the manpower barrel, and this was reflected in its members. Some were like me from the north and had benefited from reasonable nutrition and education. But more were from the south: semi-literate if at all, undernourished, and scrawny, evidencing the South's extreme impoverishment at the time even among whites (the army was strictly segregated). We contrasted sharply with the three or four German POWs assigned to work in our kitchen: big, blond, and strapping. I wondered what these thought of us in our scraggliness.

At the conclusion of four months in the sun, sand, and sweat of northern Florida amid continual sounds of rifles, machine guns, and mortars with the acrid odor of their fire drifting by, my newly acquired career interest seemed to take a turn towards realization. Along with certain other members of my company I was notified of my selection for Japanese language training at the University of Pennsylvania—this rather than being shipped off to combat in the Pacific. Germany had by this time surrendered but Japan had not. I would have welcomed Japanese language training anyway. I had a long-standing interest in the Far East through my family's participation in the nineteenth-century China Trade; in the 1850s my grandfather had visited Japan as well as China. But now, more than that, I hoped it would lead to assignments in military intelligence or the like. And these in turn would pave my way into the Foreign Service. On the troop train from Florida to Philadelphia I shared with a dozen others similarly selected an unforgettable sense of exaltation, comparable perhaps to the exaltation of the Israelites as they returned from their exile in Babylon.

Some explanation is due of how I came to be plucked in this fashion from among 50,000 or so other soldiers in Camp Blanding. This was not the first time that I had been in an Army Specialized Training Program, its official title. Prior to my infantry training I had been in an engineering program at Syracuse University, in upstate New York. Selection for these programs was based primarily on scores on aptitude tests; the army liked to do things by the numbers, and for these at least I had a knack. The programs were a hybrid of the civilian and the military. In the university's classrooms we received instruction from its professors, but we were in uniform. We marched in formation from class to class as well as to our meals; and in our "barracks," fraternity houses or civilian dormitories that the army had taken over, we were under military discipline. That I did not go on directly from this program but was detoured by way of infantry training was due to the Battle of the Bulge, the last-gasp German counteroffensive in Europe. The army contained it only by throwing all available troops into combat. But some of these troops, cooks for example, had no weapons training. Therefore Eisenhower, we were told, had decreed that all should receive it, whether they were intended for combat or not.

Stepping onto the Road

My selection did not come as a complete surprise. While in the infantry training camp I had been called in by a couple of the camp's officers to discuss my return to a university program. I told them that I hoped very much that it would be in Japanese language. They insisted that I had done so well at Syracuse University that I ought to continue in engineering (in fact I had the highest grade average in the program). Finally, however, they relented. Still this was not the end of the suspense; in the army one never knows quite what will happen. When just before the conclusion of our infantry training a list of those selected for Japanese language training was read out, my name was not on it. But a second list came through later that day. To my consummate relief, this time my name was there.

Our studies began that June. Japanese grammatical structures are often the very opposite of their English counterparts but they can be mastered through sufficient diligence. There were courses in Japanese history and culture as well. And the pressures were not so great as to preclude outside activities (Bryn Mawr, an all-women's college, was not far away). But then came August with the bombs on Hiroshima and Nagasaki and the Japanese surrender following not long afterwards. We continued in our program for the nine months originally planned, and on its completion we were sent to Japan as part of the American occupation. But by that time—April 1946—there was no longer a need for our Japanese language skills, and although we were able to use our Japanese informally, we were never called on to do so officially.

By the end of that year we were being demobilized. I, however, was reluctant to limit my experience of Japan to those months. So instead of allowing myself to be sent back to America I took my army discharge in Tokyo, where I had volunteered for a Quaker relief agency operating there. The experience turned out to be a thoroughly dismal: living in an unheated house through the Tokyo winter amid the indescribable devastation that the American firebombing had wrought and without finding anything effective to do. The surrounding countryside, also poverty-stricken, especially at that season was little more cheering. Nevertheless, my occasional visits to it provided the motif for a haiku I composed out of my discouragement.

> Through the drenching rain of winter,
> trudging over his frozen fields,
> longs the peasant unspeakably
> for the cuckoo's voice in spring.

And by spring I was experiencing a return of an adolescent depression. The responsible Quaker authorities, on being told of this, agreed that I needed to be sent home. The bright hopes for a foreign affairs career that my selection for Japanese language training had given rise to then lay in tatters.

My first months back in America were little better. I began as a factory worker in New Jersey, moving in with the family of an army buddy, but did not stay there long, rejoining my parents on Long Island for the summer. Other returning veterans found the readjustment difficult too, but I had a further disadvantage in having no real experience of civilian life. Things began to look up with my acceptance by Haverford College, which I entered the following autumn. I was given two years college credit for my Japanese language program along with my engineering program. This meant that I could graduate after only two years, although it meant also that my college education would be rather patchy. My hopes of a career in foreign affairs began to revive. I chose to major in government, which was the closest I could come to that field. The G.I. Bill would pay my expenses—thankfully, since my parents were devoid of means to meet them.

At Haverford, a Quaker institution, I graduated magna cum laude, but with the possible exception of a couple of English literature courses, nothing really excited me. Beginning as a junior, I was joining a class that had already existed for two years and most of whose members were not veterans, which made it difficult to fit in. I had attended Quaker meetings with my mother since the age of ten, and I had spent three years in a Quaker boarding school. Thus I thought of myself as a Quaker. Although I attended the Haverford Friends meeting regularly, its brand of Quakerism afforded me no great satisfaction. More fundamentally perhaps, I had not yet completed the transition to civilian life.

On graduation I still had two years of eligibility under the G.I. Bill. So I thought to use them for graduate study rather than look for a job at that time. This would give me a chance to focus on international affairs in a way that had not been possible at Haverford. I applied to the relevant graduate programs at three universities—Yale, the Fletcher School, and Harvard—and was accepted by all three. I chose to attend Harvard. During my two years at Harvard, I was much happier than I had been at Haverford. To be sure, I did not learn much; in fact, I gathered almost nothing that I found of real use in my Foreign Service career. What I eventually learned, which is most of what I know now, I learned on the job. But this is not surprising in view of the essentially craft nature of the Foreign Service. For it has its own special subject matter, with its methods of operation determined largely by that subject matter. At Harvard, I shifted my emphasis from government, my Haverford major, to economics as more likely to be of practical use. But the program I was in, concerned with international affairs generally, in contrast to the parallel Harvard programs focusing on China and the Soviet Union, offered little by way of a coherent framework. It was left largely to me to choose my courses. Further, although the professors conducting them were distinguished, among them some of the big names in economics, their emphasis was on the pre-war concepts in which they had been formed rather than on newer approaches such as that developed by John Maynard Keynes. But even Keynesian economics had limited application to the underdeveloped economies with which mainly I was to be concerned.

Admittedly, these considerations did not keep certain other members of my program from profiting. Of the twenty of us in my year, one went into domestic politics, became the Democratic whip in the House of Representatives, and was in line to become Speaker when he went down to defeat with Carter in 1980. Another became an Assistant Secretary of State. And a third, after being the ambassador to Cambodia when Indochina collapsed in 1975—and being pictured on the cover of *Newsweek*—went on to be ambassador to Denmark, Lebanon, and India. I strongly aspired to such a path myself. But had my own career followed it, I would not have been left with the space, or void if you will, into which theology, with its lasting rewards, could enter.

At the same time, I found my association with fellow students from the Graduate School of Arts and Sciences deeply gratifying, particularly in our mealtime conversations in the graduate dining hall. As for the elitist outlook that some have attributed to Harvard, it could be found even on the inside. Students from Harvard Law School joined us in the graduate dining hall, but we looked on them as able to talk only about their cases and baseball. And the Business School, across the river in Boston, we rated a notch lower still. That our rankings have held up over time may be questioned.

My second year at Harvard, however, laid an indispensable basis for my eventual turn to theology. I had spent the previous summer cycling around Europe, and on my return my father came to meet me at the boat. I was dismayed to see how much his health had slipped. This brought home to me that his end was approaching, and I felt unable to deal with this on my own. Some background is required here. My father was then seventy-eight; he had been fifty-five when I was born. Most significantly, he had lost his hearing totally and permanently at the age of six through a misguided surgical intervention. In my early years, I felt little connection with him. Communication, which was limited to his reading of our lips and our use of a rather rudimentary manual alphabet, was arduous, and he was little involved in my care. As I grew older, I found it acutely embarrassing to appear with him in public. I took his aged appearance and his difficulty in making his speech understood by those outside the family to reflect on me. But my mid-teens brought a breakthrough. I became aware, as I had not been before, of his unflagging devotion to his family even in the most difficult of circumstances. He never held my ungraciousness against me. My relationship with him became the most important that I have ever had. There was a further dimension to my theological turn. As the child of a handicapped parent, one feels a need to protect that parent, more than to be protected by him. And with his demise, this would be something that on my own I could no longer do.

Quakerism, in which I had continued, did not seem to afford the spiritual resources that I felt I needed. So in my second Harvard year, I turned to the Episcopal Church, which was my father's church and in which I had been baptized in infancy, although with my mother I had gone off to Quaker meetings later on. I began to attend Christ Church in Cambridge, off Harvard Square, and that winter I applied for confirmation. There were few people my age in the congregation, and the confirmation class was not particularly inspiring. What struck me powerfully and indelibly was the liturgy with which the Holy Communion or Eucharist was celebrated and, particularly, the Confession which it contained. I have spoken of the sense of isolation that marked my childhood. In my early adolescence this became almost unbearable, issuing in strong feelings of guilt. These had abated while I was in the army and again during my time at Harvard. But at a deeper level, they were still present. And in this Confession, which went back to Archbishop Cranmer in the sixteenth century, I heard the following.

> We acknowledge and bewail our manifold sins and wickedness . . . We do earnestly repent and are heartily sorry for these our misdoings. The remembrance of them is grievous unto us, the burden of them is intolerable . . .

This was strong language, strong enough to match any of the guilt I felt. What struck me was that not just I but everybody was saying it, moreover in the presence not only of each other but also of God. And here at a stroke my sense of isolation from God and my fellows was overcome, my guilt feelings taken away not to return. Only later did I consciously make the connection with the consecration prayer, the Great Thanksgiving with which the Eucharist climaxes.

> All glory be to thee, almighty God, our heavenly Father, for that thou of thy tender mercy didst give thy only Son our Savior Jesus Christ to suffer death upon the cross for our redemption . . .

But in some sense I must have made it even then. The lesson of my experience was that for our standing we are dependent not on ourselves but on God. And he accepts us when we turn to him, not condoning our shortcomings but not rejecting us on their account either, for which bountiful mercy our gratitude and obedience can be our only return.

I was confirmed the following spring, a few days before my father died. But he knew of it, and surely it rejoiced him.

Having received my MA degree from Harvard, I had now to find a job. Both the CIA and the State Department interviewed me, and the State Department offered me a job. It was not in the Foreign Service proper. Formally to enter the Foreign Service, I would have had to pass the Foreign Service examination. Besides, I did not want to be assigned overseas until I had acquired an American wife. This was the McCarthy era with its inquisition into any suspected disloyalty, and I feared that a foreign one might reflect unfavorably on me. Instead, the job was on the Department's civil service side. Still it substantially accorded with the career I had determined on in that formation on the Camp Blanding parade ground.

Thus I arrived in Washington in the summer of 1951. It was a tense time in foreign relations; the circumstances are worth recalling. The Cold War, which was to be the backdrop of my whole Foreign Service career, was in one of its hotter phases, particularly in the Far East. The communist take-over of China, completed just two years before, was giving rise to all sorts of apprehensions. The Korean War was still in progress, a decisive victory having been snatched from defeat through the Inchon Landing and then having evaporated in the wake of the massive Chinese intervention across the Yalu River into the north of the Korean peninsula. The memory of barely contained communist-led insurgencies in Malaya and the Philippines was recent. And the ability of the French to hold on to their Indochina colonies in the face of the determination of the Viet Cong (then known as Viet Minh) to oust them from Vietnam was becoming doubtful.

The job given me was in the Office, later Bureau, of Intelligence Research (OIR), the State Department's intelligence arm, in the Southeast Asia Branch of its Far East Division. This was staffed by a dozen analysts, most of them older than I and some of them carry-overs from the wartime Office of Strategic Services (OSS), the intelligence organization that was the precursor the CIA among other entities. They thus had a considerable leg up on me in terms of experience. Indochina, comprised of Vietnam, Cambodia, and Laos, was within our purview, as were Thailand, Indonesia, the Philippines, and Burma, countries in which also the US had a Cold War stake. Although in our office we were not directly concerned with policy, the analyses we produced could have important implications for it. Our senior analysts were in regular contact with the desk officers for our countries, whose concern it was directly. My assignment was however peripheral to all this. It was to produce surveys of manufacturing activity in these countries, initially in Thailand. Back then manufacturing was of only minor importance in any of these countries. Further, my surveys were intended only for reference, should the need for such information ever arise. Another disappointment was my immediate supervisor, whom perhaps unfairly I deemed a pedant.

This was not the only difficulty I faced at the time. The transition from the order and fellowship of student life to being on my own in a strange city was difficult, particularly socially. Several other members of my Harvard international affairs program had come to Washington at the same time, and my office colleagues were kind and hospitable. But in both groups most were already married, so that my association with them was necessarily limited. Washington reputedly had several times as many single women as single men. But most of the women had come to work for the government during the war and had then stayed on, making them significantly older. Among those in my age group the ratio was probably reversed. On some weekends I would spend hours walking around downtown Washington by myself.

In pre-air conditioned Washington, summers too were a hardship. One could escape by driving to the Blue Ridge Mountains eighty miles to the west, but on my entrance salary ($2,600 a year) I could not afford a car. The heat made for difficulty at work too. Our office was not in the main, air conditioned State Department building but instead in an adjacent former apartment house, on the top floor. There was a policy that we would be released for the rest of the day if the temperature reached 95 degrees F. (as it often did) and the humidity remained above a specified level. We would watch sweatingly but hopefully as the temperature climbed toward 95 only to see the humidity fall below that level. Together with the unglamorousness of my work, these things made for an unpromising start to my foreign relations career. But I was too young to be deterred by this.

Having recently been confirmed as an Episcopalian, in Washington I began attending Episcopal churches. If anything, they led me away from theology. In them I came up against congregations with an upper middle class composition. I sensed a separation from them in that their members had enjoyed privileges in their upbringing that I had not. To be sure, I found the preaching of the rector of one of them highly appealing. Its focus on marriage and the power of forgiveness to bring warmth to relationships was one I had not encountered before. But as I later discovered, this was of a piece with the theological liberalism prevailing at the time, consisting in giving precedence in matters of faith to human concepts over divine revelation. As such, it accorded with the upper middle class insistence on its own self-sufficiency. But human self-sufficiency over the long run is unsustainable, as its outcomes plainly show.

But my three-plus years in OIR were far from fruitless. As I came to realize eventually, they provided the basis for many of my subsequent endeavors, in the Foreign Service and in theology. Two circumstances in particular contributed to this. First, a couple of the analysts in my office were both unusually bright and deeply involved with current developments. I picked up some critical thought habits from them that I had failed to acquire in academia. Among these were checking what I read or heard against other data available to me, asking what, if something was true, would follow from it, and taking into account its implications. These procedures might be characterized as thinking both analytically and globally. Of no less value, I got to read the traffic as it was called, the classified reports coming into Washington from the embassies in the area—still sent in physically, by courier, as often as by cable. Those from Bangkok were remarkable not only for their detailed accounts of the power struggles going on in the Thai government but also for their analyses of them. They reflected of the transformation of the United States from a relatively isolated and insignificant country prior to Word War II to a leading world power thereafter. As evidenced by older reports still in the files, overseas reporting had formerly been rather diffident in its approach. Now the operative principle was never to take surface appearances, as in the pronouncements of public figures, at face value but instead to look for their underlying meaning. The new-styled reports afforded me a model for the reporting I was to do from my own overseas postings. They were also the basis for my recognition of the affinities between Foreign Service reporting and the modern biblical criticism that I encountered on entering seminary a decade later, as also for my appreciation of this criticism. For it too was concerned not so much with surface appearance as with underlying significance. And for me it opened the way into the world of the Bible, which I had had serious difficulty in entering before.

But from the standpoint both of my Foreign Service career and of my turn to theology, the most significant aspect of my OIR service was a temporary assignment to Indochina. Since the data available in Washington were insufficient for our purposes, I was sent there to write surveys of manufacturing, mainly in Vietnam but also in Cambodia and Laos. Flying out by way of Hong Kong, I arrived in Saigon in December 1952, in the midst of the conflict between the French with their modern arms and the Viet Cong relying on guerrilla tactics and on terrorism, the latter carried on not just in the countryside but also in the cities. Nothing, not even my service in the Japanese Occupation, had prepared me for the experience: Saigon's tropical lushness, the utter confusion of the wildly assorted traffic in its streets, the faded French architecture, the heavy odor of danger and decay. Near the beginning of Graham Greene's novel about Vietnam, *The Quiet American* (which was set in just this timeframe), the narrator observes that although much remains to be learned, after only fifteen minutes there one understands things in a way not otherwise possible. I can endorse this observation.

But I still had to produce the surveys that were the object of my assignment. The question was where, amid the welter of impressions crowding in upon me, to begin. Available statistics even in the field were few and unreliable, even for such industries as existed—light ones like matches and soap manufacturing with some textiles in the north. So I had to come up with most of the figures myself. The only way to do this was by going to the managers of factories, mainly still French. But most of them did not speak much English and I wondered, would they be willing to talk to me anyway? The limitations of my French at the time were such that I had to listen with complete attention to understand them. However, this seemed to convey that I was really interested in what they had to say, and so to dispose them to speak freely. As a priest I have found this same attentiveness to be of key importance in pastoral counselling.

Stepping onto the Road

The information I was able to collect in this way only partly resolved the main problem. This was how to reduce all this strangeness and confusion to meaningful patterns in the reports I was to write. Initially, I tried to apply the concepts that consciously or unconsciously I had brought with me from the West. Try as I would, though, they never really fit. I went through a period of no small distress on this account. Finally, instead of attempting to impose my own patterns on the data, I took the risk of allowing the patterns to emerge from the data themselves. And then things began to fall into place. This was a significant discovery, and not just for my subsequent functioning in the Foreign Service. It accords with a dictum of Francis Bacon, the English lawyer-philosopher of the late sixteenth and early seventeenth centuries who laid much of the basis for modern science. Voltaire, the leading *philosophe* of the French Enlightenment, in fact termed Francis Bacon the hinge of the modern period. This dictum was, "We cannot command nature except by obeying her." Nor is its significance confined to the natural sciences. In that it implies that the methods of a science need to be determined by its own subject matter and not by *a priori* considerations, it justifies the claim of theology to be a science. I have found it to be indispensable in my approach to Scripture. When in preparing a sermon I try to interpret the passage I am preaching on in accordance with what I think it ought to say, I do not get very far. Only when I allow meaning to emerge from within it does it become luminous.

My Indochina assignment, mainly in Vietnam but also in Cambodia and Laos, got me thinking seriously about going on to the Foreign Service proper. Although I found the Indochina environment sufficiently exciting, my assignment there had limited policy relevance. On top of this, I had bouts of intestinal illness—a regular hazard in the tropics. Thus I might not have been sufficiently impelled towards the Foreign Service except for a particular circumstance. Back in Washington an important strategic question had arisen. This was where the Viet Cong were getting their military supplies and equipment. China, adjacent to Vietnam, had come under communist control but imports from there were still not significant. And Vietnam was deemed to lack the facilities to produce them. While in Saigon I happened to get wind of a defector from the Viet Cong who had been the director of industrial production in one of their "resistance zones." He was now located in Central Vietnam, in the city of Hue, under French control. I managed to go there to talk with him and a couple of his associates who had come over with him. He had a remarkable story to tell: mortars made out of salvaged cast iron, explosives derived from bat droppings in caves, bicycles pressed into service for the transport of supplies—Peugeot bicycles, which prevailed in Indochina at the time, my informant characterized as *assez solides*. Even more impressive was the degree to which the population had been mobilized, not just in support of the war effort but also in the avoidance of practices such as smoking which might detract from it. My report on this was regarded in the embassy, in the State Department, and even in the Pentagon as contributing to filling this intelligence gap. This result persuaded me finally that my future lay in serving overseas.

GUARD TOWER: During their phase of the Vietnam War, from about 1947 to 1955, the French built many guard towers along the country's rural roads. One of them figured prominently in Graham Greene's 1952 novel, *The Quiet American,* and also in the 2002 movie version. By the time of filming, however, all these guard towers had disappeared, necessitating the construction of a copy. Here is one of the originals, in 1953.

My temporary assignment in Indochina was decisive in another way too, although this did not become apparent until later on. In Saigon there was an Anglican congregation of no more than a half dozen members, services being led by a young lay reader from the British embassy. When I heard of it, I began attending, and I found it to be the one place where amid all the confusing strangeness of Vietnam I felt at home. The impression it made on me was abiding.

Back in Washington my work in OIR continued much as before. Then a year or so later what had been a major cause of my hesitation about entering the Foreign Service was removed. I met an American girl whom I liked very much, moreover one from the rock-ribbed state of Utah, whose loyalty Senator McCarthy could scarcely impugn. Following our marriage, some time later I applied to take the highly competitive Foreign Service exam. This consisted of two parts, a written and an oral section. I took the written one and did very well. Still, I doubted my ability to pass the oral one; I thought I lacked the necessary verbal agility and self-confidence. But taking the oral was rendered unnecessary. At just that time a program was instituted, called the Wriston Program, whereby entrance could be made laterally from the civil service into the Foreign Service. I availed myself of that. By the end of 1954, eight months after our marriage, I was scheduled to go overseas on a regular assignment. On the form for listing my post preferences I had put Cambodia first, as offering promising work opportunities without some of the stresses to be encountered in Vietnam. Presently, word came from personnel offering me that post. I accepted immediately. Surely this time the aspiration that had come to me on the parade ground at Camp Blanding a decade before was being fulfilled.

2

A Plethora of Potholes

THINGS DID NOT TURN out at all as I had anticipated. Instead, from the standpoint of my Foreign Service career, my first three postings were calamitous, bringing it to the edge of failure. Whether or not one does well in an overseas assignment depends on more than one's competence and dedication; other factors come in to play, for example, how critical the country is to United States interests at the time, or the particular responsibilities that one is given. The most important factor, however, is one's supervisor—the leadership provided as well as the cogency of the annual efficiency reports written by this person, which are virtually the sole basis for promotion. In my first post, my supervisor was a bad fit for his job as well as disagreeable personally. In my second, my supervisor was, I am obliged to say, a disgrace to the Foreign Service. And in my third, I was effectively without supervision, which in some ways was the worst situation of all. Thus the way was impeded not only to my advancement but also to my acquisition of the vital disciplines that distinctively the Foreign Service affords. With sufficient determination and application I might have surmounted even these obstacles, but I was still deficient in these attributes. It was these same three postings, however, which set me on the path to ordination and thus to a full engagement with theology. My ordination was an outcome that previously I would have found inconceivable. Further, apart from the particular circumstances of these postings it almost certainly would not have come about. In the end, it was my engagement with theology that mattered.

As already mentioned, soon after my transition from civil, or domestic, to Foreign Service had gone through, I was offered an assignment to Cambodia, to the embassy in Phnom Penh. This was a better outcome than I had expected. In making my survey of manufacturing in Indochina I had visited Cambodia and been attracted by its relative tranquillity—under King Sihanouk it remained mostly untouched by the fighting in Vietnam. At the same time, it seemed to offer a chance to make a mark. Accordingly, I had listed Cambodia as my first post preference (one was asked to list them on becoming eligible for an overseas assignment). But only a few days after I had accepted the offer, I got a phone call from the Personnel Office saying that the assignment had been switched—to Saigon (Personnel was not above employing bait and switch when it came to positions at posts that were "difficult and dangerous" and thus not easy to fill). I was less than happy about this but having committed myself to going overseas I had little recourse. So after packing our belongings for either shipment or storage, my wife and I headed out to Vietnam, arriving in January 1955.

When I had left Saigon two years before, there seemed still to be a reasonable chance that the French could overcome the Viet Cong insurgency and keep Vietnam in non-communist hands, thus minimizing the communist threat to the other two Indochina countries and to Southeast Asia in general. But now the Vietnamese jig seemed to be about up. In 1954 the French, having unwisely gambled on being able to hold the northern outpost of Dien Bien Phu, had thrown in the towel, negotiating a settlement with the Viet Cong. This entailed the division of the country into two halves, north and south, and the withdrawal of the French. When we arrived, they had already completed this in the south and were proceeding with it in the north. In the settlement the north was to be given over to the Viet Cong. The south was assigned provisionally to the government of Ngo Dinh Diem, a nationalist rather than a communist but untried as a national leader. Its ultimate disposition, however, was to be determined by a referendum in 1956, in which everyone expected the Viet Cong to prevail. There was no American military presence at the time and thus no one to evacuate us in case the Diem government should collapse. Its prospects were even more tenuous than I have indicated. Non-communist but dissident factions dominated the countryside: the Hoa Hao, the Binh Xuyen, the Cao Dai. Diem's control was limited essentially to Saigon itself, and even within the city the national police adhered to the Binh Xuyen. Their headquarters was a building on the city's main street. In walking down it one was careful to pass by on the other side.

Amazingly, Diem was able to assert his control over the whole of the south. But this was only after a pitched battle with the dissidents fought in Saigon itself. One evening soon after our arrival my wife and I were startled by the explosion of mortar rounds fired at Diem's presidential palace a mile or so away. A day or two later, a lively skirmish took place just blocks from the house where we were living; I was then at the embassy but my wife was there. The main fighting, however, took place in the eastern part of the city, known as Cholon. Some of us went up on the embassy roof to observe the clouds of smoke rising from it. We did not stay long, though, for bullets began to whistle around us. Within days, however, Diem's forces prevailed and began to extend their reach into the countryside. Unfortunately I was unable to savor their victory, as just then I came down with amoebic dysentery and had to be evacuated to the American base at Clark Field in the Philippines for treatment.

As for my job, I was assigned, appropriately, to the embassy's economic section. It was at first headed by an able and congenial officer, Hoyt Price by name, under whose tutelage I think I could have prospered. However, he left shortly and his replacement was a very different story. Evidently he had had no long career the Foreign Service but had come in through a political connection. His background was in the private sector, in banking or finance, and he brought that mind set to Vietnam. Although the condition of the overwhelmingly agricultural economy of South Vietnam—price stability, supplies of rice and other foodstuffs for the cities—surely bore on the ability of the Diem government to hold on, he showed little interest in these things. His attention seemed to be almost entirely on the establishment of a legal framework for South Vietnam's new central bank. This was the main area to which he assigned me despite my expressions of interest in agriculture. But I did not have sufficient technical knowledge to be effective in it, nor did he provide me with guidance. As for the above view of his personality, it was not mine alone. His predecessor, whom I happened to run into some years later, spoke of him to me as a "sour apple." My Saigon tour had been set for two years, the normal length. But was reduced to one when my wife developed a need for surgery which could be performed only if she returned to the United States. At the time this could be arranged only by transferring me back to Washington, so I was transferred.

A Plethora of Potholes

While back there I discovered what sort of efficiency report my supervisor had given to me for my time in Saigon. I had not seen it at post, and even in Washington under the regulations existing at the time I was not allowed to read it but only to have it read to me. It was not only highly critical but contained substantial inaccuracies as well. I could and did write a rebuttal on the basis of what I could remember of it. But the promotion panel which considered it is unlikely to have given what I said much weight. Needless to say, this was not auspicious for my future in the Foreign Service.

In the long run, however, the significance of this Saigon tour lay in what it brought about for me theologically. As already related, when I had been in Saigon before I had attended the services held by the small Anglican congregation there and found them to be of great value. On again arriving in Saigon one of the first things I did was to see if they were still going on. They were, but the young officer from the British embassy serving as its lay reader was soon to be transferred, with no replacement in sight. To my surprise—I had never done anything of the sort before—the British ambassador, who was one of the congregation's regulars, asked me if I would be the lay reader's replacement. I hesitated. It would mean tying myself down on weekends, which on account of my hopes for recreation I was reluctant to do. On the other hand, if I did not step in, the congregation would go by the board. And that seemed a worse outcome. So with my wife's encouragement I accepted, so that as lay reader (eventually licensed by the Bishop of Singapore) I led the services of evening prayer. For these services, as before we used the building of the French Protestant church, which continued to be available to us on Sunday evening, the French congregation needing it only in the morning.

The military and political situation in the ensuing months continued to be tense; even after the battle in Saigon that I have described the final outcome remained uncertain. And getting to the services involved braving the hazards of Saigon traffic, which were formidable. Yet our services continued regularly all through this time. Attendance, which had been only five or six, including my wife and the British ambassador, rose to about twenty. Previously, I had never thought of ordained ministry; had someone broached the idea to me then I would have dismissed it out of hand. But by the time I had to leave Saigon, the idea had come to me of pursuing ordination, not immediately to be sure but after my retirement from the Foreign Service.

FRENCH PROTESTANT CHURCH: This building in central Saigon was shared with the Anglicans by a local French Protestant congregation. As was reflected in the previous chapter and as will be further reflected in the next, the building played a key role in the author's call to ordained ministry.

Back in Washington my wife's surgery was quickly and successfully performed. We had to hang around, though, until our medical clearances came through. Then we got our next assignment; it was to the American consulate in Sydney, Australia. Perhaps this was intended to give us a respite from the rigors of Saigon. But Australia, with all its peace and order, was no match for the excitement of Vietnam. As with Vietnam, one needed actually to be there to appreciate what the country was like. Although its climate was reasonably temperate, it was subtlety different from that of America or Europe. Instead of a clear progression of the four seasons, there was a continual shifting back and forth, as with one day being spring-like but the next blazing hot. The vastness of the island/continent—about the same size as the contiguous United States—in relation to its population, then only about twelve million, was also disconcerting. The coastal areas, where all the main cities were located, were habitable enough, and the portions of the interior where rainfall was sufficient supported large-scale production of wheat and wool, still among the mainstays of the economy. But the central part was a vast, unreclaimable desert. A geologically ancient land, its eons-long isolation from other land masses was reflected in its flora—eucalyptus trees predominated—and its fauna—all native species, the kangaroos, the koalas, and even the Tasmanian tigers, were marsupials. And at that time evidences of past cultural isolation were still to be felt. On occasion, Sydney made me think of a mid-western American city a decade or two earlier.

Of more immediate professional consequence was the country's relation to US policy interests. It was peripheral, not because it was unimportant but because of the extent to which it could be taken for granted. Far from threatening to go communist (although it had a lively labor movement), it could be counted on as a United States ally without any special efforts being made to keep it so. And such issues as might arise between the two countries were dealt with by the embassy in Canberra, the capital, not in Sydney. Commercial representation and visa issuance were virtually the only matters left to the consulate. I had a stint at the latter but mainly was concerned with the former. Thus the scope for retrieving my performance record from the blow it had been dealt in Saigon was decidedly limited.

Even the possibility of this turned out to be precluded, through a repeat of my Saigon experience with my supervisors. The supervisor on hand when I arrived, Bob Cleveland, was able and congenial and I think would have viewed my performance favorably. But he left soon after. And his successor, so far as I could see, was a dud. His background was not in the Foreign Service proper. Instead, he had come into it on the basis of having served as an agricultural attaché. Even in the Foreign Service, his outlook remained profoundly rustic. Nor was this the worst of it, not by far. Noting that I had a talent for writing and evidently aware that he did not, he made me a proposal. It was that instead of my name being on the reports back to Washington that I wrote, he would put his own. This meant that the credit for them would go to him rather than to me. In return, he promised me a favorable efficiency report. This of course was in flagrant violation of Foreign Service rules and ethics. But at the time the system afforded me no ready recourse; only later was such provided for. I needed a good report if I was to get out of the hole that my Saigon tour had put me in. Further, my wife had at last achieved the conception that we had been ardently hoping for. But her pregnancy was a delicate one, and I was anxious to avoid subjecting her to any special stresses. So I accepted the supervisor's proposition, despite all my misgivings. As time went on, however, I became increasingly uncomfortable with it; it made me feel as if I were all the time wearing dirty underwear. Finally, I told him that I could no longer abide by it. He did not say much in response but, waiting until after I had left Sydney, he wrote an efficiency report that panned my performance. Again, I wrote a rebuttal but again it was unlikely to have carried much weight. Thus my promotion deficit was enhanced instead of being overcome.

My wife's pregnancy was maintained and our older son was born in Sydney, two and a half months before our tour was up. His birth was in a modern hospital such as would not have been available to us in Saigon or elsewhere in the less developed world. However, this was not quite the offset to my professional setbacks that it might have been. In this hospital he contracted a staphylococcus infection from which he became gravely ill. And my wife contracted it from him, so that she had to be rehospitalized herself. We had little idea how to care for a newborn anyway. The strain of this situation, on top of what had befallen me in the office, almost put both of us under.

As for my turn to theology, Sydney did not do much to advance it. My wife and I attended a parish church near the suburb where we lived, but I derived no particular insights from it. I still might mention that the vicar, when towards the end of my stay I told him of my eventual interest in ordination, presented me with a copy of the Greek New Testament, which evidently he did not use himself. This made no sense to me; at the time I did not know even the Greek alphabet. But within four years I was learning New Testament Greek. And from that I have gone on to read the Scriptures in Greek and/or Hebrew daily now for fifty years.

Having left Australia as a hot summer was ending, we returned to Washington to catch the beginning of a hot summer there. And only at its end did we go overseas again. It was a difficult time, lodged as we were in a transient apartment with no air conditioning and the necessity of taking care there of our infant son. During that time, though, something curious occurred. Rather than having our son baptized while we were still in Australia, we had decided to wait until we got back to Washington. It could then take place at the church that I had been attending. When the day came, we drove into the city from our apartment and found a parking place a few blocks from the church. As I carried our son down the avenue to it, suddenly there flashed in my mind the account of the Sacrifice of Isaac, in Jewish tradition the *Akida*, wherein Abraham sets out to sacrifice his only son in obedience to the Lord's command. Then, at the last minute, he is told to hold his hand. There was no apparent reason for this account to present itself to me; I had not yet been to seminary nor was it a story that I was particularly familiar with. I thought later that this might have been because the passage (Genesis 22:1–19) reflected the way in baptism we give our children over to the Lord, although I have not seen this interpretation applied to it. Perhaps also it was a foreshadowing of what was to overtake our son later.

On our arrival back in Washington we had been told that our next post would be Baghdad. From its climate and its rather primitive facilities it appeared not to be an easy place to live. In fact, the post report made it sound dismal. I was not dismayed, though. I thought that in the Middle East, a region which was even then of considerable interest to US policy, I might have a chance to retrieve my performance deficit. Before we could set out, however, the existing government of Nuri Pasha was overthrown in a coup—the one that paved the way for Saddam Hussein—and the assignment had to be cancelled. Instead, it was decided that we should go to Karachi, then the capital of Pakistan, where I would be not in the embassy but on detail to AID (more recently USAID), the American economic development agency. After my Baghdad assignment fell through, Personnel perhaps did not know what else to do with me. At any rate, I never got a proper explanation of why I was being sent there or what I was to do once I arrived. We did not leave Washington immediately because the Pakistan desk officer, to whom I was temporarily assigned, kept extending my time on the desk. But finally, I boarded a plane for Karachi with my wife and son.

We arrived in Karachi just over a decade after the centuries-long British rule of the subcontinent ended in its partition into the two states of India and Pakistan. The partition, along the lines of the Hindu-Muslim divide, had been horrendous, bringing about massive transfers of people in both directions accompanied by endemic violence and bloodshed. This was evident in the large numbers of refugees from India still living in flimsy structures on the roadsides. In part, this reflected the dire poverty of the country. Its economy was mainly agricultural but its agricultural potential was seriously limited. Its West Wing—it still had the East Wing which later was to be Bangla Desh—consisted of the Desert of Sind, abutting on Karachi, and Baluchistan and the other Northwest Frontier provinces, rugged in topography as well as in people. The Punjab, farther to the east, was more hospitable but even there agriculture was heavily dependent on irrigation from the Indus River. Moreover, defects in the design of the irrigation system had resulted in extensive waterlogging and salinization. The scarcity of resources had not however precluded the maintenance of a large army, then as now the dominant element in the country. Its position had been reinforced by a military coup just at the time of our arrival, installing General Ayoub Khan as president. The US interest in Pakistan was mainly as a counterbalance to India, which at the time was prominent among the countries professing to be non-aligned but showing receptivity to Soviet overtures. Underlying this interest was, of course, the Cold War rivalry with the Soviet Union.

Karachi is on the Pakistan coast as well as on the edge of the Desert of Sindh, enabling it to become a major port city. In Karachi there had not been any rain for a year and a half, and there was not to be any for another year. The dust along the streets was inches thick. But the Indian sub-continent has its fascinations, which we were glad to experience despite the trying climate and the illnesses that recurrently struck us and, particularly, our infant son. It was an exposure to a non-western culture such as I had not had before. In the Karachi area with its desert conditions, its numerous camels and donkeys even on the city streets, and its sheep and goats on the hillsides, one seemed to get a glimpse of Old Testament times. Later I was to find that biblical passages, particularly from the Old Testament, would take on a clearer meaning when viewed against this background.

Given the predominance of agriculture in the economy and the predominantly rural character of the population, AID's activities in Pakistan were devoted largely to agricultural technical assistance and rural development. I was assigned to the mission's program office, which performed essentially an accounting function. It focused on previous and anticipated funding for the various assistance projects and their Personnel requirements. The forms generated in the process were used not only in administering these projects but also in justifying them in the annual budget submissions to Congress. They provided relatively little scope for analysis of the relation of these projects to the larger economy. Judging by questions asked in the budget hearings, Congress did not have much interest in their relationship anyway. Thus there was not much scope for overall economic analysis such as was customary in embassies, the sort that accorded with my underlying interests. Just as I had not been able to get any clear explanation of the purpose of my AID detail, so the program office did not have much idea of what to do with me. Other than some routine checking of the forms, little was asked of me. I made some efforts to break out of these constraints. I produced some critiques—probably not very tactful—of the rural development program, and I undertook to promote an inductive approach to the data, the principle that had proved crucial in the survey of manufacturing Indochina that I had carried out several years before. But a framework such as would have made the relevance of these efforts evident was lacking. Nor did I apply myself very thoroughly to comprehending the intricacies of the accounting procedures. In the Program Office, I found no lack of good will on the part of its members. In these circumstances, though, its director did not have much basis for the efficiency reports that he was required to write on me.

The precariousness of my situation was brought home by a letter from Personnel notifying me that my performance had put me only a step from the selection-out zone. It may have been my Harvard degree that kept me from going over the line. I thought that I still had the possibility of retrieving my career in future postings; if my Harvard degree had saved me once it could save me again. The uncertainty of the assignment process and my own persisting lack of an analytical framework for my perceptions in fact augured against this. At this stage, though, I had not taken such things fully into account and so was not unduly dismayed by this notification.

There was, however, a strong theological countercurrent to the above adversities during my time in Pakistan, one that might not have run so strongly had my official duties been more absorbing. Karachi had an Anglican church dating from British times, still with plaques commemorating various British army regiments on its walls. My wife and I attended its services and sometimes I was asked to read one of the lessons. The vicar was a New Zealander and the congregation was still mainly expatriate—not the case any more. Its significance was not so much in itself as in the bishop under whose jurisdiction it came, a convert from Hinduism rather than the prevailing Islam but still a Pakistani. Technically the assistant Bishop of Lahore in the Punjab, he was resident in Karachi and had responsibility for the congregations there and in the adjoining province of Sindh, which though mostly a desert was habitable in the valley of the Indus River. He was perhaps the most gifted preacher that up to then I had heard, and he preached often in our church. More than that, he allowed me to sit in on meetings with rural church leaders and took me to visit some of their villages. I was astonished by what I found. The villagers were, of course, extremely poor, and the leaders at first sight were not very impressive. But there they were, standing firmly in their faith despite their poverty and their status as a small island in a forbidding Muslim sea. In both respects they were quite unlike the Christians of the west, affluent and with a secure place in society; rather, they were like the Christians of Roman times. Through my exposure to them, somehow I saw the reality of the church as I never had, and never would have, had I remained only in the west.

The experience impacted me profoundly. It did not lead to an immediate spiritual transformation on my part; I retained the essentially worldly outlook typical of my associates at work. But it caused my idea of seeking ordination to move from the distant future, after my Foreign Service retirement, to the near present. This, of course, would be no small step. It raised the question of how, in the absence of a salary during the requisite three years of seminary training, I was to support my family and myself. But after some calculations I decided that our savings with some outside assistance might just do. I broached the idea to my wife. She was scarcely enthusiastic, but she did not strongly object.

But there was more to it than that. I could not just decide on my own to go to seminary. I would need to be endorsed by my parish church back in Washington, to be accepted by the diocese as a postulant, and finally to be accepted as a student by the seminary itself. After completing my tour in Pakistan, instead of being sent overseas again I was given a Washington assignment, back in OIR but dealing with central and south Asia instead of with Southeast Asia as before. This gave me a chance to obtain the assent of the parish and the diocese and also to gain admission to a seminary in the Washington area, so that my family and I would not have to move. My hope was to go on leave without pay from the Foreign Service; I could then come back in if my time at the seminary did not work out. But my application to do so was not granted. Accordingly, I had to resign from the Foreign Service, my resignation becoming effective shortly before classes at the seminary began.

3

Seminary: Agony and Ecstasy

The seminary I attended was divided within and even against itself, a division which turned out to be programmatic for the subsequent history of the church. Nominally it was centered on the proclamation of the gospel, the traditional and essential vocation of any Christian seminary, and some of its courses still accorded with this center. In practice, however, it emphasized another center, namely secularly-derived "pastoral theology." Traditional studies, in particular those relating to the Bible, church history, and systematic theology, continued alongside it. But their relation to it was left unclear, relegating them to a secondary position. For most of the students, the new center was the one that counted—hence the longer-term consequences for the church. For me, the attraction lay in biblical studies and church history, in the subjects themselves and in their affinity with my Foreign Service experience and disciplines. But I did not feel that I should or could ignore the pastoral theology side, psychotherapeutically-centered though it was. And this side engendered confusion in me as well as in the church, in which I continued for many years. For this and other reasons, seminary did not end my difficulties. Instead, I ran up there against new ones, which were harbingers of greater to come. Thankfully, though, enough of the seminary's traditional vocation remained to bring me, after many trials and much tribulation, to a comprehension of the biblical gospel. And it was at seminary that the links between my Foreign Service career and theology first struck me, powerfully. These have been the basis for any contribution that I can make to theology, as also for this book.

First, a note about my transition from Foreign Service to seminary: It was no small shock to the system. Having been out of classrooms for ten years, I took a while to get used to sitting through the hour of a lecture. My fellow students, in a class of about sixty, were mostly younger than I and without professional experience such as I had had. On this account, the lasting relationships that I formed were with faculty members. No less a part of the transition was a sharp reduction in the family standard of living. I received some financial assistance along the way, but I had to meet the larger part of the cost of seminary out of savings. By the time I completed the three years of training these savings were mostly gone.

I need now to account for the divide within the seminary, the oldest and the largest of those affiliated with the Episcopal Church. It had a tradition of being evangelical, that is, of having confidence in the power of the biblical tradition to reach people and to bring them to faith in Christ. But perhaps through an insufficient understanding of this tradition, it had come largely to lose this confidence. For had it allowed itself to be taken over by the above "pastoral theology," an approach based not on the gospel but instead on secular principles, in particular those of the psychotherapy then in vogue with its emphasis on the surfacing of repressed feelings. Thus most of its students came away with the impression that the use of psychotherapeutical techniques in managing congregations as well as in counselling parishioners was "where it was at." The proclamation of the gospel remained for them a nebulous enterprise. To be sure, the seminary had its theologians, its lecturers in systematic theology, a couple of them well reputed. They did not partake of the seminary's psychotherapeutic turn; to some extent, they even stood against it. But they refrained from doing so openly, perhaps because of their reluctance to take issue with seminary colleagues, perhaps also because liberal tendencies in their own theology had deprived them of a sufficient basis for doing so. In formal terms, they could be said to have leaned towards Paul Tillich rather than towards Karl Barth—which tendency may have contributed to the seminary's loss of evangelical confidence.

As acknowledged, I emerged confused on these points. By virtue of my exposure to the real world in the Foreign Service, I had some sense of the artificiality of pastoral theology, of the limitation of its applicability to affluent individualistic societies in the West. But I had come to seminary with still rudimentary ideas of my particular vocation, and only later did I become sufficiently clear about it to question the seminary's orientation. In any case the seminary afforded me access to the its traditional elements, its evangelical side, which I found not so much in systematic theology as in biblical studies and church history. The lecturers in them—Murray Newman, Holt Graham, and John Booty deserve to be named—were not all of them great scholars. But they were imbued with their subjects to the point of being able to impart their enthusiasm. Moreover, these were the studies for which my Foreign Service experience had specially prepared me. But the negative side of the seminary is also integral to the story. Therefore, it should also be told.

The formal courses in pastoral theology were not oppressive. In fact, they introduced me to some valuable ideas: those of Paul Tournier, the renowned Swiss psychologist, and of Jean Piaget, the discerner of childhood patterns of cognitive development. It was in the summer programs of "clinical training" that the sharp edges revealed themselves. The one that I took part in during my first of my two summers was in a general hospital, the one during the second in a semi-rural parish setting (those in greatest vogue among the students were in psychiatric hospitals). The exposure of seminarians to actual people, away from classrooms, was commendable in principle but deficient in practice. In the hospital we dealt with patients who were seriously, even terminally, ill. But the larger part of our time was spent in discussions with our supervisor. These discussions were devoted not to relating our hospital experiences to the gospel—though the biblical tradition provides abundant materials for doing this—but to digging out our inner feelings, as of anxiety, unresolved conflict, or anger, especially anger. By getting in touch with them we were supposed to be enabled to get in touch with the feelings of the patients with whom we dealt, thereby bringing about their salvation. In the Foreign Service, by contrast, the emphasis is on sublimating individual feelings into overarching purposes. There was indeed merit in this exercise; such feelings are vividly recognized in the biblical psalms, which thereby are adapted to this very function. But what was not appreciated, and what I myself did not then appreciate, was that simply bringing out feelings is not enough. Unless there is a framework in which to set these feelings once they have been brought out, bringing them out is rather like throwing a tennis ball. To this one finds little resistance but from throwing it there is little effect. The only adequate framework for so setting them, as I was later to discover, is the biblical tradition and what can be seen to follow from it. Thus the approach we were employing could not bring real comfort to the patients with whom we were dealing. Neither could it give us a sense of serving a power larger than ourselves and, in so doing, of being empowered by it.

If this first summer program missed the mark, the second one was downright destructive. It was supervised by a priest who had trained at the same seminary some years before, when pastoral theology held its greatest sway there. He had become committed to it to the extent that he excluded almost everything else. He showed no great interest in our experiences in the parishes to which we were assigned and in which we spent most of our time. Instead, his concern was evidently to assert psychological dominion over our group. His methods could be brutal. During one of our sessions with him, my wife phoned him to say that our young son had come down with German measles and a high fever and that she urgently needed our car to take him to a doctor. He neglected to get the message to me. Our son recovered despite this but with possible long-term effects. When, on another occasion, I unintentionally crossed him, he called me "common" (he pronounced it *cormon*, he was from the South), tearing off his clerical collar as he did so. It must have been by grace that I survived.

This summer program was significant probably in showing how readily the pastoral theology emphasis on surfacing feelings can devolve into an exercise in power. Indeed, it could not help so devolving given its premise that psychological force was necessary to bring feelings to the surface, people being inherently resistant to their surfacing. And this required that the applier of the force be in a position of power, as was particularly the case with supervisors of seminarians, who as such are inherently vulnerable. Actually, the exercise would have been more detrimental to the wielders of this power than to those over whom they wielded it, given that power exerted apart from God is necessarily corrupting. This seems to have been the case with the supervisor of our program. I ran into him some years later. He was then a florist displaying his wares in the State Department building, of all places. Evidently the extremity of his methods had led to his breakdown as a priest. There was a further deficiency in the approach that he and his like took. This was their failure to recognize the power of the biblical tradition to loosen people's resistance to bringing out their repressed feelings, so that they can be surfaced fruitfully, without distortion. That the biblical tradition together with its sequel in the history of the church has this power was to be one of my principal theological discoveries.

Seminary: Agony and Ecstasy

I should note that subsequently the seminary moved away from its psychotherapeutical emphasis, more than it had prior to my own time there. But this did not entail a reversion to the centrality of the gospel. Instead, other secularly based emphases took its place there as they did also in the wider church, deriving from "social justice" without much reference to the gospel. Indeed, they essentially became the gospel, the hard edge with which they have been pursued being perhaps the legacy of the psychotherapy formerly emphasised. In one of his parables Jesus tells of an evil spirit going out of a man only to wander in dry places and then deciding to return to the house from which it had come, bringing with it seven spirits more evil than itself. And finding the man's house "swept and garnished," they enter and dwell there, so that the last state of the man is worse than the first (Matthew 12:43–45 and Luke 11:24–26). The decline of mainline denominations, the Episcopal and others, in recent years may be seen an instantiation of this parable in our time.

But as I have said, my biblical and historical studies at the seminary were another matter. Not only did my Foreign Service experience turn out to be directly applicable to them, they opened vast new vistas for me. To be sure, I did not immediately comprehend these vistas—far from it. Here, though, I will describe them as they subsequently unfolded, for only in this way can their already present germ be made comprehensible. Further, in their developed form they illuminate events still some years off, for which they were the basis.

The fullness of these vistas was foreshadowed already in an experience I had a couple of weeks after arriving at seminary. It was in my introductory New Testament course. The lecturer, after beginning with some preliminary considerations, had us turn to the Gospel according to Mark. Scholars generally regard Mark as the first of the four New Testament accounts of the life, death, and resurrection of Jesus to be written down, albeit this did not happen until the latter 60s of the first century. He then led us through Mark's first chapter verse by verse. As he did so he asked what an ordinary Roman of the first century would have made of these verses (the scholarly consensus is that Mark came out of the Christian community in Rome). As he proceeded, it came home to me that my own cultural standpoint, which I had always taken for granted, was not the only one from which to view the biblical accounts. There was in fact another and more appropriate one, namely that of their first readers or hearers (many of the early Christians were illiterate). As this realization dawned, it was as if scales fell from my eyes. For the first time, I saw these accounts no longer just in black and white but instead in their original vivid colors. They came alive for me as they never had before—an experience of Pentecostal proportions.

What happened to me was consistent with the potential afforded by modern biblical criticism: the application to the Scriptures of analytical procedures such as are employed in the natural sciences and various other fields of investigation. Biblical criticism already had a considerable history but it had developed especially in the preceding decades. Among its fruits was the recognition that the historical books of the Old and New Testaments, including the Gospels, were for the most part not first-hand accounts. Instead, they had circulated in oral form for a number of years before being written down. Thus they were in some degree shaped by the communities that had preserved them in this form. What impelled these communities to preserve them was the importance they held for them, as necessary not just for their holding together but also for their survival in the face of the extreme difficulties confronting them. These would have included the threat and actuality of conquest and exile in the case of the Old Testament community and severe hardship and massive persecution in the case of that of the New. Indications of these concerns are to be found by looking not so much at the surfaces of the biblical accounts as beneath them. And when so looked at these accounts take on an additional dimension and a compelling quality. Indeed, only when we see what they meant for those for whom they were first written down does it become possible fully to see what they mean for us—as I found to be the case with the first chapter of Mark.

Most notably, I was struck by the affinity between this approach and the one I had come upon in OIR, when I first joined the State Department. There I was able to read the political reporting from the embassies in Thailand and elsewhere in Southeast Asia. And I found that in this reporting the pronouncements of public figures were not taken at face value either. Instead, they were probed for their underlying motivations; as in biblical criticism the texts were probed for what lay beneath the surface. In academic circles this is known as applying to them a hermeneutic of suspicion—itself regarded with suspicion in certain quarters. I think those who do so underrate the inherent power of the Scriptures, which under assault emerge stronger than before.

Additionally, I found that approaching the Scriptures in this critical way called for the full employment of my critical faculties. Thus I would not need to leave behind those I had developed in the Foreign Service but instead would need to draw on them to the full—a crucial point for me. Moreover, in these things I saw the possibility of effective communication between the two thought-worlds, that of the church and that of the Foreign Service—and not of the Foreign Service only but also of other secular professions and occupations. And, coming out of this possibility, I saw a breath of new life fill the church. It would be my special vocation to contribute so far as I could to its realization.

Predisposing me to an acceptance of modern biblical criticism with its emphasis on the communities out of which the Scriptures came was my Foreign Service exposure to non-Western cultures, as in Pakistan. For these cultures are closer to those of the biblical peoples than is our modern Western one. Abraham, Isaac, and Jacob, and the wilderness wanderings of the Israelites, when viewed in against a Pakistani background—deserts, camels, tough-looking tribesmen—take on a color and definition they do not otherwise have. But arriving at what the eyes of the biblical peoples, or those of a first-century Roman, would have seen does not take place of itself. It requires bringing to bear on them the geographical, historical and social circumstances of the ancient peoples and the implications of these for their life-situations. For this also the Foreign Service, in which I needed to bring similar considerations to bear on the situations that I was analyzing and reporting, provided a valuable preparation.

I should not omit to speak of finding in my overseas postings that if I spoke to people in their own language, even a few words, they would become open, their faces would light up, as they would not otherwise. On arriving at seminary it occurred to me that if I learned the biblical languages, Hebrew and Greek, the Scriptures might similarly open themselves. So, unlike most of my classmates, I studied both. My supposition turned out to be fully warranted. Biblical translations, valuable as they are, can never have quite the force and clarity of the original texts. Indeed, it is only on the original texts that the tools of critical analysis can be brought fully to bear. And it is the power of these texts that has kept me reading the Bible in Greek and/or Hebrew daily for more than fifty years. Indeed, I cannot imagine starting a day without doing so.

My discovery of modern biblical criticism had an important personal dimension. Since my adolescence, I had taken the Scriptures seriously but without ever being able to get quite into them. An obstacle I kept running up against was their miracles: could such things really have happened? Biblical criticism became my means to set it aside. An aspect of this was my seminary-acquired awareness that instead of distinguishing between an event and its meaning, as we regularly do, the ancients tended to combine the two into a single account. Unless allowance is made for this, the biblical miracles may indeed be baffling. Further, the ancients' concern was not so much with the "factuality" of an event (our modern concept of "fact" is itself open to question) as with its ability to convey the power of God. Especially as I read them in the biblical languages, the accounts of miracles took on this power for me.

As will become apparent later in this book, a biblical insight that came to me while at seminary but outside its precincts turned out to be critical. It came as much through the analytical faculties that I had developed in the Foreign Service as through my seminary-acquired knowledge. As part of my training I, like my fellow students, served as the seminarian at a church—this one in northwest Washington. In this capacity, I took part in its services, including the celebration of Pentecost one year. My assignment was to read the Epistle for the day, the account of the first Pentecost in the second chapter of the Book of Acts. It tells how on the Jewish feast of Pentecost fifty days after Jesus' resurrection his disciples assembled together. The Holy Spirit then descended on their gathering, impelling them to go out from the room where they were meeting and proclaim the wonderful works of God. Bystanders heard them speaking in the languages of their origin. The passage gives a lengthy list of their nationalities: Parthians, Medes, Elamites, and others sounding even more exotic to us, but would not have so sounded to residents of the ancient Mediterranean world. Herein was the inception of the church's outreach, beyond the disciples' own circle to the world itself.

My assignment was given to me only minutes before the service began. Thus I had no time to sort out how these exotic names were pronounced. I decided that instead of slurring them over so as to obscure my ignorance, I would speak them boldly, as if I knew what I was talking about. Afterwards, a young lady in the congregation remarked on how impressive the list had sounded. This got me thinking. It struck me that whatever happened in Jerusalem that day, the list of nationalities could well have represented the peoples to whom the gospel had spread by the time the Acts account was written down—probably in the latter first century. On this basis, the special intelligibility of the disciples' speech would signify the way in which these peoples had received the gospel—as if expressed in their native languages, their most intimate possession. And this supposition, for which there is support in the Acts account, would go far to explain the almost incredible rapidity with which the gospel spread in the ancient world. Further, it would indicate that if the gospel is to be received now as it was then, the terms in which it is expressed need to be consonant with thought patterns of modern professions and occupations—such as the Foreign Service. This insight validated for me the affinity between Foreign Service disciplines and modern biblical criticism that had so struck me at the outset of my seminary training. Moreover, in this affinity, and the basis for communication between the church and the world that it afforded, I saw new possibilities opening for the church, indeed a new Pentecost.

A basic link of the Scriptures with my Foreign Service formation needs also to be noted. It is afforded by their concreteness: the situations one analyzes in reporting from overseas back to Washington are similarly concrete. Concreteness, which is significant in itself (cf. the discussion of crafts in chapter 9), is the mark of history, not only of the history in the making that the Foreign Service is concerned with but also of that of past. And the Scriptures consist basically of history. To be sure, there are considerable sections of theological reflection, as in the Psalms and Job in the Old Testament and the letters of Paul and others in the New Testament. But what they reflect on is this history: the history of salvation or the history which itself is saving. It is highly dramatic, as can be appreciated by those who have had experience of critical situations overseas. To convey both its concreteness and its drama, I will now set out a considerable outline of biblical history, the fascination of which was already apparent to me at seminary.

The Old Testament begins with accounts, metaphorical rather than literal, of the creation of the world out of nothing by God's word, of the fall of Adam and through him of humanity when in the Garden of Eden he attempted to transcend his human limitations, and of the migration to Egypt of the descendants of Abraham—the story of humanity's redemption from Adam's fall begins with Abraham. Old Testament history in the usual sense of history may be taken as having its inception in the Exodus: the escape of the Israelites, as they came to be known, from their slavery in Egypt. After years of "hard service in brick and mortar," under Moses' leadership they managed to flee their taskmasters and Pharaoh. At the Red Sea (in Hebrew simply *yam suph* or sea of reeds) they found themselves trapped by Pharaoh's pursuing army. Their predicament confronted them inescapably with their human powerlessness. But they were unwilling, or unable, to accept it. So they turned on Moses, demanding why had he led them to perish in

Theology and the Disciplines of the Foreign Service

the wilderness. To Moses, however, it was given to accept this powerlessness and in it to turn to the Lord, declaring to the people, "Fear not, stand fast, and you will see the salvation of the Lord which he will preform for you this day" (Exodus 14:15). And the Lord delivered them, parting the sea (whether directly or by the east wind blowing all night which the Exodus account also speaks of), so that the Israelites—but not the pursuing Egyptians—were able to cross it. Through this, the event of their deliverance, the Lord became the Israelites' God and they became his people. This relationship was made explicit in the covenant granted by the Lord through Moses at Mount Sinai. Only in terms of this covenant is the subsequent history of Israel, Old and New Testament, intelligible.

The Israelites did not enter the Promised Land immediately; instead they wandered for forty years in the wilderness. Even then they could take possession of it only by conquering the Canaanites, the previous inhabitants. But having done so they found their loose confederation under threat by neighboring peoples, notably the Philistines who nearly did them in. Out of this critical struggle came the centralizing monarchy, under first Saul and then David, in whose reign the Philistine menace subsided and other foes were subdued. (The biblical account of David's kingship, its internal as well as its external politics, is remarkably circumstantial, lending itself to the sort of analysis that a Foreign Service officer could have sent back to Washington.) Solomon, David's son, on his accession took over what amounted to a small empire. But evidently he became bedazzled by his own greatness, to the point of losing the sense of human powerlessness that had enabled Moses and also his father David to turn to the Lord. In Solomon's son, Rehoboam, this loss was complete. The conditions he thought he could impose on his people were so harsh as to drive the northern half of the country to secede. Thereafter, there were two Israelite kingdoms, a northern and a southern. Though they remained able to ward off many of the assaults of their smaller neighbors, in their division they were ill positioned to resist the rising superpowers of their time, first Assyria and then Babylon. Perhaps they could not have anyway. The outcome was the Assyrian extinction of the northern kingdom in 722 BC and the destruction of Jerusalem and the exile of the people by the Babylonians in 586.

To complete my account of Old Testament history I will need to speak of an insight that did not come to me while at seminary even in germ but only during a subsequent Foreign Service assignment in Vietnam. In brief, it was that the essential role of prophets—Amos, Isaiah, Hosea, Jeremiah, and the others—was not to predict the future or to rebuke the people for their sinfulness. Instead, it was to preserve the validity of the covenant, to maintain its framework of meaning in the face of the catastrophes visited on Israel by the Assyrians and the Babylonians. This insight cannot properly be appreciated apart from the particular circumstances out of which it arose. So I will reserve a full account for chapter 5, concerning my final tour in Vietnam.

This outline of Old Testament history may seem to downplay a major element of it, namely the role of David and of the monarchy which, following the stumbling of Saul, David put firmly in place. Surely this was an important component but perhaps not quite in the way usually thought. From a Foreign Service standpoint David's significance may be seen not so much in the exemplarity of his faith as in the widening of Israel's horizons which his political and military achievements enabled, opening the people's imaginations to the larger implications of their covenant relation with the Lord. One of these implications was that they would be delivered from their afflictions later on, notable among them their subjection to Rome, through a Messiah who was to come.

In the New Testament, history is more narrowly focused than in the Old, but it is no less significant for that. This history is regarded as the culmination of Israel's history, towards which all of that history points. It centers on the life, death, and resurrection of Jesus, the Messiah who did come into the covenantal framework that the prophets had preserved. He came, though, not as the warrior leader to deliver Israel from its Roman occupiers, the expectation of whom the Davidic tradition had given rise to. Instead it was as one without worldly power, going about with his disciples to teach and to heal. This did not however keep opposition to him from arising within Israel. On the contrary, it caused the religious establishment to regard him as a threat (my own sensitivity to the role of the establishments derives from experience of them in the Foreign Service). Therefore they would have to eliminate him. Even then he neither drew back from confrontation nor offered them any material opposition. The outcome was his death on a Roman cross. Thus while drawing on the messianic tradition stemming from David, he diverged from it, conforming rather to the figure of the suffering servant spoken of by the prophet Isaiah (53:3–4).

> Surely he has borne our griefs and carried our sorrows
>
> yet we esteemed him stricken, smitten by God and afflicted.

> But he was wounded for our transgression, he was bruised for our iniquities;
>
> upon him was the chastisement that made us whole, and with his stripes we are healed.

But the story does not end there. It takes a turn completely unexpected even by his disciples. For in the midst of their despair over his death they witnessed his resurrection, God's raising him from the dead. The implications of this are stunning. Indeed, they change the way one thinks about everything. The authors of the Gospels chronicling Jesus' earthly ministry as well as the writers of the New Testament Epistles undertook their elucidation. However, it fell chiefly to Paul, the former persecutor of the Christians, who grasped them in all the novelty of their implications and in his letters articulated them with utter daring. To him was due also much of the early spread of the church, as tirelessly in his far-flung missionary journeys he proclaimed the good news of Jesus Christ.

The content of this good news or gospel—gospel means good news—was essentially that by raising Jesus after his death on the cross, God had transformed his apparent defeat by the powers of this world into no less than his victory over the sin and death which had entered humanity through Adam's disobedience in the Garden. Moreover, through Jesus' sacrifice of himself, this victory was now available to all who believed in him. As for the connection between the powers of this world and sin and death, this was left perhaps more implicit than explicit. But it can be discerned through an examination of the nature of establishments such as the Jewish religious one and the Roman secular one. They are not totally negative in their functioning. Indeed, they can play exceptionally positive roles; otherwise they could not gain their ascendancy. But in this positive side lies a profound ambiguity. It puts them in a position of power beyond that of other worldly entities. They are then tempted to regard themselves as self-sufficient, as no longer dependent on any power beyond themselves, as a power unto themselves. They regularly fall into this temptation, just as Adam fell in aspiring to take God's knowledge of good and evil upon himself. Thus establishments are wont to become the primary embodiments of the death-entailing original sin ascribed to Adam. And Jesus' victory over them, through his allowing their apparent defeat of him, thus constitutes his victory over sin and death, for himself and for the entire world. This victory, together with the surpassing joy that it brings, is the supreme triumph that is celebrated at Easter.

Seminary: Agony and Ecstasy

To be sure, the biblical history is of a special kind, one that has been given the name of salvation history. But it has strong affinities with the events, the history in the making, with which the Foreign Service deals. In many ways, the Scriptures were new to me, but I felt that in this respect I was in continuity with what I had been doing in the Foreign Service.

Continuity with the Foreign Service was a feature also of my studies in church history. They pertained largely to the early church and to the Reformation, both of them subjects that appealed to me personally in that they spoke to my Foreign Service experience. Nor was my appropriation of them entirely subjective. My term paper on the early church and its martyrs received a grade of A++ [sic], and an essay I wrote on Archbishop Cranmer and the English Reformation was chosen for discussion by the seminary's faculty book club. To make the continuity of these studies with the Foreign Service comprehensible, I will need to include insights that came to me not at seminary but only after long reflection. But as with my biblical insights, similarly continuous with my Foreign Service experience, they were already present in germ.

The story of the early church, from its inception at the Pentecost event (described above) to the issuance of a decree of toleration in the year 311 by the Roman Emperor Constantine, seemed marvelous me. In less than three centuries, it spread from Jesus' immediate followers in Jerusalem, mostly illiterate, throughout the empire, moreover in the absence of all modern means of communication. In doing so, it attracted massive opposition, especially on the part of the Roman élite. But in the end it was the church not the state that prevailed.

As for the church's spread, it can be seen as coming to a significant extent from the nature of Roman society. Analyzing this society in terms applicable to Foreign Service reporting is fruitful. The Romans began as a small nation in west-central Italy that was involved in a struggle for sheer survival with their neighboring peoples. The discipline and organizational talents that they developed in this struggle enabled them first to take over the rest of the Italian peninsula, then, after defeating Carthage, the whole Mediterranean littoral, and finally, most of western and northern Europe. In its own discipline, its insistence on getting things done no matter what the cost, the Foreign Service provides a good basis for this insight into ancient Rome. In the process, though, Roman society underwent profound changes. From being essentially egalitarian, having its mainstay in small-scale plebeian farmers, it went to being strongly hierarchical, dominated by a patrician class based on large agricultural estates, or latifundia. Politically, the change was marked by the shift from republic to empire. It was powered by the acquisition in the course of the Roman conquests of vast numbers of captives, whom the patricians made use of as slaves to operate their holdings, thereby displacing the plebeian farmers. These, along with the slaves, amounted to the main part of the population. This part may be said to have been in but not of society, as such constituting a proletariat.

The treatment of the slaves, in the Roman mines and on the monumental construction projects as well as on the latifundia, was harsh. It accorded with Roman mind-set to regard them solely as a means to an end, without value as human beings. Nor did they have material hope of escaping their condition. The great slave revolts—climaxing in the one led by Spartacus in 73 BC—all failed. Thus nothing was left to the slaves except to internalize the worthlessness attributed to them, to regard themselves as having no inherent value. In contrast, the church reckoned them as worthy, as those for whom God's own Son had died. The church's valuation enabled them to overcome their internalization of worthlessness as nothing else could have, enabled them to stand upright in the face of the forces crushing them psychologically as well as physically—hence, the church's particular appeal to them and to others similarly disregarded in the Roman dispensation. From those so disregarded came most of the church's converts.

The opposition to the church was mostly unofficial in the beginning. It came partly from rival religious sects, from artisans and others with a stake in the idol-worship which the church displaced, and from mobs easily incited against it. But more and more, it became official, directed by the Roman authorities. And from being confined to particular cities or provinces it went to being empire-wide, as in the persecution under the Emperor Decius in the year 252 or the final climactic persecution under the Emperor Diocletian in the years 309 to 311. In effect, the state did its utmost to wipe the church out. This was despite the church's consistent abiding by Roman laws—its members even paying their taxes—and its unwavering adherence to non-violence in the face of the violence directed against it.

The question arises: why this opposition? The answer appears to lie in the spiritual liberation afforded by the church's faith. The hold of the Roman authorities on their subjects was in part physical, through the threat or use of the force of which they possessed a monopoly. It was also psychological, operating through the majesty of empire, which the authorities were at pains to render unquestionable. The church, however, was constituted on a different basis, independent of the state, namely the lordship of Christ rather than Caesar. Further, in the obedience its members rendered it there was no element of coercion. Instead, given the likely cost of their membership, this had to come out of their own commitment. And by standing on this ground, the church called into question the bases of empire, exposing the essential insecurity of a system based in the last analysis on force. Thus the state, in all its panoply, felt threatened by the church as it felt threatened by no barbarian hordes.

In the end, however, it was the church rather than the state that prevailed. How could this be, given that in its attempt to eliminate the church the state employed all the means at its disposal, not just the extremes of physical repression but also psychological techniques of great subtlety? To be specific, in the times of persecution all the people were required to offer incense or some other sacrifice to Caesar (by this time the Roman emperor was considered a god). If they complied, as non-Christians readily could, no further questions would be asked. If they refused, they would be subjected to the most horrible tortures, ending in death. We might suppose that in sacrificing with mental reservations we would not have unduly compromised our faith. The church understood that it could not acquiesce without undercutting its allegiance to Christ, thereby negating its gospel and relegating its members to their previous spiritual bondage. Not all of them stood fast in the face of what they were subjected to, but large numbers did. Evidences of this are the white-robed army spoken of in the *Te Deum,* and also the great multitude that no one could number spoken of in Revelation 7:9. The book of Revelation is best understood as coming out of such a time of persecution. Both relate to the church's martyrs. In the face of their fortitude—many who saw it were converted, spreading the church even more—the Roman rulers saw that they could not be forced to renounce Christ. Thus it was that they issued their edict of toleration, their acknowledgment finally that for all their superiority of force they could not overcome the church. This highly improbable outcome is epitomized in no less than the cross. The Romans in choosing it as their means of execution intended to inflict not only maximum agony but utter degradation on the condemned. Yet by Jesus' crucifixion it was transformed into the symbol of triumph over all the powers of the world.

For me, the martyrs had a special significance. As noted, Roman society was highly stratified, with slaves and many others being regarded as of little or no value. In parallel to this, the hierarchical nature of the Foreign

Service lends itself to the equation of official rank with personal worth. In the martyrs' light I saw the extent to which I had internalized the value that my persisting low Foreign Service rank assigned to me. I saw also that where the early church's martyrs had stood firm against their socially ascribed value—this in the face of the most daunting pressures—I had not so stood. I had to confess how far I had fallen short

In saying these things am I contradicting the merit that I have attributed to the Foreign Service's disciplines? I do not think so. Instead I have been pointing to the paradoxical nature of all institutions, how they provide the framework within which one can be creative, how they call forth this creativity but at the same time act to stifle it. As for the resolution of this paradox, it is not to be sought in the Foreign Service or any other such organization. Instead, it lies beyond all such entities, in theology.

The Reformation was the other area of church history that I found especially appealing, particularly the English Reformation. An aspect of its unfolding was the same organizational duality discernible in the ancient Roman state—a calling forth of talents but at the same time a stifling them—as also in the Foreign Service. There was a further reason for my interest. In chapter 1, I described the life-change that I experienced on exposure to the Anglican Eucharistic liturgy with its unequivocal acknowledgement of human guilt, how it lifted from me my deep-seated feelings of isolation and guilt, permanently. At the time, I knew little of the source of this liturgy. Through my seminary studies, though, I learned the story behind it, a story that was deeply meaningful for me.

The English Reformation differed from those in Germany and Switzerland in that it was initiated not by Reformers like Luther, Zwingli, or Calvin but by the king, Henry VIII. Further, he acted not so much out of theological principle as of dynastic politics: the need he felt for a male heir. Thus in England the Reformation lay under a cloud; a question existed as to its validity from the standpoint of faith. And this cloud would have persisted, the question of its validity would have gone unresolved, had not been for the part played by Henry's Archbishop of Canterbury.

Henry's story has been told before. When his queen, Catherine of Aragon, produced a daughter but no son, he petitioned the pope for a divorce from her so that by remarrying he could improve his prospects of obtaining one. But the pope refused him. His response was to cut the English church's ties to the papacy, thrusting aside those who, like Thomas More, could not in conscience relinquish their papal allegiance. What is not so well known is the appropriation of Henry's action by the considerable number in England who had been inspired by the continental Reformation and who earnestly desired to institute it at home. Without their support, Henry probably could not have pulled it off.

Among those so inspired was a young and obscure Cambridge cleric, Thomas Cranmer. He had come to Henry's attention before the final break with Rome through an essay providing a theological justification for Henry's divorce. Henry, sensing his potential, elevated him in short order to be Archbishop of Canterbury, the senior prelate in the English church. Cranmer responded to his elevation with an unquestioning loyalty despite Henry's frustrations of many of Cranmer's aspirations for ecclesiastical reform. Notable among these aspirations was changing the liturgy from the traditional Latin into English, the language "understanded of the people." Edward VI, the son that Jane Seymour had produced, succeeded Henry. Edward, however, was only nine years old at the time. He was also somewhat sickly, so that governing fell to a royal council of which Cranmer was a member. In this position, he was able to carry out the reforms that he had long desired, notably producing a liturgy in English that has endured to this day.

Edward died at age fifteen. The succession fell to Catherine of Aragon's daughter Mary, who was ruthless in returning the English church to its Roman obedience. Cranmer's position became a delicate one, to say the least. He kept his peace as long as he could, but in the end, he burst out with a condemnation of the restored Roman mass. This resulted in his arrest and confinement in the Tower of London. While he was imprisoned, he wavered, writing a series of recantations of the positions that he had taken. However, these were not sufficient. Cranmer was brought to Oxford to be tried in the University Church (pictured on cover) and condemned, like many others in Mary's reign, to be burned at the stake. The ignominy of this outcome is inescapable. However, as the flames rose around him, he thrust his right hand, the instrument of his recantations, into them saying, "This hand hath signed, therefore it must burn first." And he held it there steadily until it was consumed. His gesture, at the last possible moment, somehow redeems him from his ignominy, elevates him to the ranks of the saints and martyrs.

The organization in which Cranmer served was the Tudor monarchy, which did not end with the death of Mary but continued under Elizabeth, Henry's daughter by Anne Boleyn. It can be seen how much the Tudor monarchy called forth Cranmer's talents but also stifled them. That in his character there was considerable weakness is evident, first in his uncritical loyalty to Henry and then, despite his initial defiance, in his caving to Mary and signing his recantations. Yet the power was given to him even so to transcend the organization to which he had committed himself. If Cranmer, in his weakness, could thus be redeemed, so could I in mine.

This, then, was my experience of my seminary. It was incoherent, to be sure; however, along with bitter fruits it bore some exceptionally sweet ones, moreover bearing great promise of future fulfilment. Finally, after three years exceptionally arduous for my family as well as for me, I graduated, prepared presumably for parish ministry. The question, then, was what would happen next.

4
A Highly Incongruous Parish

THE NEXT STEP WAS my ordination to the diaconate—one serves as a deacon for some time before becoming a priest. It took place a couple of weeks after my seminary graduation, in the vastness of the Washington cathedral. Several of my classmates were ordained with me, and the attendance by family and friends was considerable. Ordaining us was the assistant bishop of the diocese. A Marine Corps veteran who as a priest had engaged in inner city ministries, he cut an impressive figure; later, though, the ambiguity of his life emerged. But in the church's tradition the validity of its ministrations is not determined by the worthiness of the minister. When my turn came to have his ordaining hands laid on my head, the seriousness of what I was entering into hit me as it not had before. Once I went forward there would be no turning back, whatever the outcome might be. I went forward anyway.

I have already spoken of the duality of the seminary I attended; on the one hand, it provided the materials out of which a deep understanding of the Christian gospel could develop, but on the other, it fostered approaches sharply divergent from that gospel. Its provisions could thus be characterized as deeply ambiguous, a combination of the very positive with the very negative. But there was not much ambiguity about the year that I spent full-time in a parish, following my graduation. The negative elements that had been present at the seminary predominated; the hazards that I had been exposed to there came at me in full force. They had serious consequences for my family and me. In part, they were the result of coincidental circumstances but mainly they came out of a lapsed condition of the church. As for whether my undergoing these consequences served a purpose, ordination, which occasioned them, was my gateway to theology, and from that standpoint they were a necessary cost. Further, in the world, fallen as it is, one expects to run into such hazards. But fallenness is present also in the church. To turn aside from the church would be to leave it without a means of restoration and thus unable to address the world's fallenness. Ordination itself should not be undertaken apart from realities like those to which people in the church's pews are exposed, in all their ambiguity.

The date of my ordination was among the coincidental circumstances productive of hazards. Following World War II there had been an upsurge in church attendance, enjoyed by the mainline denominations generally. The war had fostered a sense of national unity, of being caught up as a people in a common purpose. The church had lent itself to this purpose and in doing so had become the object of renewed interest, being seen as relevant to what was going on in the world after all. This interest, in which the wide attention attracted by the writings of the theologian Reinhold Niebuhr played a part, carried over into the post-war period. When I entered seminary in 1961, the growth in attendance was expected to continue, and the seminaries were taking in correspondingly large numbers of students. By the time I graduated, however, it had halted, as post-war euphoria waned and people became preoccupied with the Cold War and various other international and domestic problems. In the light of these problems, the theologically liberal message that most churches were offering at the time came to be seen as lacking.

On account of these developments, the placement of seminary graduates in parishes, their normal destination, became difficult. Such positions as were left for them to be assigned to were generally the less desirable ones. The diocese, having accepted me for training and having duly ordained me as a deacon, was supposed to find a position for me or, as last resort, to release me to find it for myself—not an enviable prospect. The diocese came up with a stopgap for me rather than an ongoing position. For the summer, I was placed in the Washington cathedral, where my main function was leading visitors on tours of the building. It struck me that the cathedral—which conveyed the transcendence of God in its soaring dimensions and the central concepts of creation, judgment, and redemption as portrayed in its stained glass and stone—had an unusual potential to convey Christianity to these visitors. But my discernment of this potential did not lead very far, for me or for the cathedral. I found its leaders little disposed to exploit it. Evidently, they had not fully grasped the biblical imperative to proclaim the gospel. Accordingly, they were content to let the cathedral be treated largely as another tourist attraction.

At the end of the summer, however, a chance came to move on from the cathedral. The rector of church in northwest Washington stopped by to invite me to be his curate, offering a one-year contract that I trusted would be renewed. Thus the problem of my on-going employment, following my assignment to the cathedral, seemed to be resolved. More than that, this curacy would give me a chance to gain experience of parish ministry, to demonstrate my talent for it, and perhaps to be called to be rector of a church myself. But my expectations went unfulfilled. This church turned out to be a singularly unpropitious place for the beginning of an ordained ministry, or perhaps for any point in it. I can characterize it only as dismal. The difficulty was not with the members of the congregation; there were good people among them. Rather, the main reason was the rector himself.

I had not been acquainted with him beforehand, nor he with me. He was an older man—though not as old as I am now. He had been that church's rector for most of his ordained ministry, and he had never had a secular profession. He was not into psychotherapy; it had not been a seminary emphasis in his day as it was in mine. But such ideas as he had were distinctly old-style, representative perhaps of a previous era against which the psychotherapeutic vogue I encountered at seminary had been a reaction. He had no deep knowledge of either theology or the biblical tradition. His preaching consisted basically of the conventional wisdom, conforming the gospel to it rather than it to the gospel. As such, it was conducive not to challenging the congregation but to keeping them content. Nor was he inclined to let his curate outshine him. As for his mindset, a counseling session that he told me about was I think representative. A woman in the congregation, pretty and quite young, had come to him saying that she was having sex with a somewhat older man and asking his advice. He advised her against it on two grounds: she might get pregnant and she might get caught. Evidently he did not think to tell her about the Christian view of marriage as ordained by God and as symbolizing "the mystical union that is betwixt Christ and his church," how sexual relations within it can lead to joy but outside it can confer no blessing. A ministry of his sort, however amiable, could only be regarded as destructive. Certainly, it afforded no valid guidance for me. Of course, the main loss was that of the rector himself, who in his failure to apprehend the real gospel missed out on its excitement. If he failed because the real gospel was not adequately presented to him at seminary, the incoherence now to be seen in the church as well as the seminary may be regarded as having arisen prior to the psychotherapeutic vogue, and not just with it.

In the parish, I had to contend not only with the rector but also with the vestry, the body elected by the congregation to make financial decisions and otherwise oversee its administration, thus having considerable power over the clergy. As within its jurisdiction, the issue of housing, which the parish was supposed to provide for my family and me, came before it. While I was at seminary we lived in an apartment not far from its campus. But that was in northern Virginia, not in northwest Washington where the parish was located. Continuing to live there meant a lengthy daily commute for me, and for my family it meant doing without transportation during the day; we had only one car. As the months went by we found this situation increasingly difficult. Eventually, we came upon an available house in the vicinity of church but at a considerably higher rent than our apartment. For financial reasons, the vestry would have preferred that we remain in Virginia; the parish's finances were rather tight. But I pressed the point, and I prevailed, though at the cost of alienating a key vestry member.

More decisively, in the parish the psychotherapeutic approach, which I had thought to leave behind at the seminary, caught up with me. As described previously, by the time I arrived at my seminary, it had already somewhat shifted from its previous strong emphasis on this approach. But the clergy who had been trained there in the preceding years for the most part had not. There were several of them in the diocese, its young Turks, and they were intent on propagating this emphasis and, not incidentally, their own position in it. To these ends they devised and presented to the bishop what they called a deacons' training program for those newly ordained—as noted, ordination is initially to the diaconate and only subsequently to the priesthood. They justified it on the grounds that without it these deacons could not be effective in their parishes. And the bishop, himself evidently lacking a strong Christian compass, accepted their proposition. I had no choice but to participate, along with my fellow deacons—some nine of us. In the year following ordination, one continues to be highly vulnerable. The program, which required attendance at day-long sessions away from our parishes every other week, reproduced some of the worst features of the summer programs

A Highly Incongruous Parish

I had been in at seminary. One of them was the endless navel-gazing into which the program's directors prodded us, warning that without being in touch with our feelings we could not successfully manage our congregations or counsel our parishioners. The program's basis was essentially secular; its references to the gospel consisted mainly in the transposition of theological concepts into psychoanalytic ones. What it came down to essentially was an exercise in power. Apparently, I did not show sufficient enthusiasm. Shortly before I was due to be ordained to the priesthood, which was six months after my ordination to the diaconate, its director called me in and told me that "unless you get your ass into therapy" I would not be priested. I might not have been except that a fellow member of the program, of whom I had no expectation of such a thing, wrote persuasively to the bishop on my behalf. Even so, my standing with the rector and the vestry was damaged and my position in the parish made more tenuous.

In the Foreign Service also one may be subjected to rough treatment. But it at least tends to be in line with the underlying mission of the institution and so can and frequently does have positive effects. This training program, however, involved a divergence from what on historical or any other reasonable grounds had to be the church's essential vocation: the proclamation of the gospel. Thus it could lead only to futility, for the clergy undergoing it and for the church itself.

As for what I did in the parish, I was given considerable opportunity to preach, to conduct services, and to lead classes and discussion groups; I cannot fault the rector on that score. In view of the potential of the ideas I had developed at the seminary for opening communication between the church and the world, I might have been expected to do well in these activities. But at the time I had not given them their requisite focus, and I made only a limited impression with them. The parish hazards I have been describing certainly contributed to my inability. My own inadequacies were also important. I had still not overcome the lack of self-assurance arising, as noted in chapter 1, from the circumstances of my childhood, nor was the fact that in my first year of ordination I was on probation in an unfamiliar setting conducive to doing so. However great the potential of my ideas, I was still far from being able to articulate them as I did in the previous chapter. I also had not really grasped their relevance to the proclamation of the gospel or how to draw on them in connection with it. Further, I shared in the confusion of the seminary and also the wider church over their essential vocation. To a significant extent my own ideas had become submerged in the psychotherapeutic rationales that had been impressed on me, more than the gospel, as the core of ministry. Moreover, subscription to them had been held out as the route to a successful church career such as would be required for the support of my family and me, and I had no clear grounds for questioning this notion.

Still another factor contributed to my inadequacies. In chapter 2, I spoke of the deficiencies of my three overseas postings prior to entering seminary, how they provided me with very limited guidance and experience. As a result, I was not yet fully formed in the Foreign Service. I had not developed the steadiness of application, the critical and analytical skills, and the clarity about one's objectives essential to effectiveness in a parish as well as in the Foreign Service. Moreover, my curacy in that parish afforded few chances for developing these attributes. Short of further Foreign Service exposure, and this of a truly rigorous and relevant kind, it seemed that I might never do so.

I was both delivered from this impasse and afforded the requisite further Foreign Service exposure. My deliverance came about through a development that at first seemed disastrous, and in fact it entailed a heavy cost. It may nevertheless be regarded as providential. The reprieve from losing my job afforded me by being after all ordained a priest did not endure. As the year specified in my contract as curate approached its end, I heard nothing about its renewal. Finally I went to the rector and put the question to him. He then told me that it would not be renewed. This put my family and me in a desperate financial situation. At seminary, we had run through most of our savings, and even in the parish my stipend—$5,000 a year—was not fully covering our expenses. I cast about frantically for another church position but none was available to me, at least not anywhere near Washington. I had left seminary fully expecting to spend the rest of my career in parish ministry. But now the only possibility of employment lay in getting back into the Foreign Service. I doubted that I could do this, but it turned out that I could—provided I was willing to be sent to Vietnam. The American build-up, civilian as well as military, was then at its height, and positions, especially for those with previous experience of the country, were available. But this meant family separation; the assignment was considered too dangerous for dependents and none were allowed. I would have to leave my wife and our then-seven-year-old son behind. I was deeply torn by this prospect, with ample reason as it turned out. However, I felt that I had no choice but to accept it. Thus in October 1965, I flew out to Saigon for a tour there of a year and a half.

My parish year did not end in total defeat, however. When word of the non-renewal of my contract got out, twenty members of the congregation took it upon themselves to petition the bishop that it be renewed after all. His response was that he was not unwilling but that he could not, since authority in the matter was solely the rector's. He did, however, authorize me to go into non-stipendiary ministry, as it is termed. I had feared that after leaving the parish I could no longer function in the church as a priest. His authorization meant that I could, though, even while deriving my income from secular employment. In this, I was something of a pioneer. Non-stipendiary ministry was rare at the time, but subsequently it became fairly frequent.

Beyond this, as my farewell in the parish I was permitted to conduct a service of Evening Prayer. I included in it a recitation of the ancient canticle, *Nunc Dimittis*:

> Lord, now lettest thou thy servant depart in peace,
> according to the word.
> For mine eyes have seen thy salvation
> which thou hast prepared before the face of all people,
> To be a light to lighten the gentiles
> and to be the glory of thy people Israel.

Evidently my recitation deeply impressed the congregation. And it had the effect, which I had not intended, of moving my wife to tears.

An addendum to my account of my year in this parish may be in order here. I have characterized the deacons' training program I underwent in unremittingly negative terms. Thus it might appropriately be asked how the program could have been turned around—how it could have been refashioned to accord with the principles we have here been adhering to, so as to be a blessing instead of a curse. This is a critical question. The shadow of program did not fall just on us deacons as we underwent it. It fell also on our trainers who, in their determined pursuit of their own objectives, missed out on the joyful obedience to the gospel that they might otherwise have known.

First and foremost, the program would have had to be established on a very different basis. Its actual basis, as here described, was psychoanalysis and the techniques to which it gave rise, a secular approach which has since been seen to fall short even by secular standards. Instead, its basis would have been the biblical gospel: centered in Christ, spelled out in the Scriptures, and deployed in the sacraments, history, creeds, and doctrines of the church. These two contrasting bases, the improper and the proper, align respectively with two very different objectives for the program. Our trainers made protestations to the contrary. Nevertheless the only purpose the actual program could hope to serve was to equip us deacons to dominate our congregations. For the mastery of a group, the constraining of its members into a mold, was essentially the role that our trainers were modeling for us. In the absence of a transcendent purpose, an overarching goal—for there was none apart from the enhancement of our clerical status and income—this could lead only to a dead end for our congregations and for us. The second basis would, however, have provided for the conveying of the good news of Christ, not just to our congregations but to those beyond them as well. In this case, instead of being closed in on ourselves, we would have had our horizons opened ever more widely. In meeting the resulting challenges we would have had access to the whole biblical tradition, deployed as above, as our resource. We would have had the gratification of serving not just ourselves but a far greater cause; in fact, the greatest of all.

This is not to say that everything in our ministries would then have gone smoothly; such is not the way things work in this world. But instead of having to look within ourselves for the resources to meet the difficulties we encountered, we could have looked to the Scriptures and to our obedience to them. The Scriptures do not, of course, have prescriptions for all possible contingencies. But it is the case that when we are sufficiently imbued with them, images from them will arise spontaneously in our minds to match the circumstances with which we are confronted. This is not just a matter of my personal testimony. When Jesus was tempted by the devil at the beginning of his ministry, in each instance he responded out of Scripture (Matthew 4:1–11 and Luke 4:1–13). As they provided him, the images from Scripture provide us with what we need in order to respond.

This second basis, the proper one, would have entailed our meeting regularly as a group, as in the actual deacons' program. In so meeting, in addition to Scripture study and sacramental celebration—the actual deacons' program lacked even prayer—we could have shared the difficulties we were encountering along with the biblical images that might have arisen in our minds under their impact. This sharing would have given us the benefit of the experiences of our fellow deacons and, likely, would have enhanced our appreciation of our own. Supervision of these meetings by established clergy would have been appropriate, provided the supervisors were grounded in Scripture as well as experienced in parish ministry. In fact, it would have been important as a means for channeling the discussions so that they were disciplined by the Scriptures rather than conformed to the world's concepts, while at the same time being in touch with the realities of parish ministry. If pursued along these lines, our discussions could have been relevant existentially, dealing with our involvements with rectors and congregations. They would not have been conducted abstractly, in isolation from these involvements, as was the case with the actual deacons' program.

An alternative program such this would not have been without historical precedent. In the Puritan tradition arising in the wake of the Reformation, the institution of the presbytery or *classis* was developed, consisting of a grouping of churches in a particular locality. In England, under Queen Elizabeth I, many clergy who were Anglican but nevertheless favored the Reformed or Puritan emphasis met in *classes* for biblically centered mutual correction and encouragement. Such an institution would have much to offer also today, not just for deacons but also for other clergy and for lay people.

5

Again in Vietnam

SAIGON AT THAT TIME was singularly well suited for making up what was lacking in my Foreign Service formation. In fact my tour there played a pivotal role in this formation and in my theological formation as well. Not only that, it afforded me a chance to continue functioning as a priest, as I was intent on doing. And its special circumstances opened to me a dimension of the biblical tradition which otherwise I might never have grasped. It did, however, entail a personal cost.

In many ways I was glad to be back into the Foreign Service, even apart from the return it meant to gainful employment and ability to support my family. I remember my satisfaction at getting my hands on classified documents again, at the connectedness with important happenings in the world. There was also the renewed association with people of the sort with whom I had previously worked, the opportunity once more to be a meaningful part of a team. My year of parish ministry, which pre-eminently should have afforded this, had not done so; but then my previous Foreign Service assignments had not either. To be sure, the prospect of being in Saigon again was a little daunting. There was the debilitating climate to contend with and the exposure to tropical diseases. A few months before I arrived, the American embassy had been blown up by a car bomb; the Viet Cong may have pioneered the technique. There were frequent attacks against civilian as well as military targets, terrorism continuing to be a major Viet Cong weapon. But I had survived my previous times there, and I could presumably do so again.

My main concern about going was the family separation that it necessitated. Except at the highest level, no dependents were allowed. My wife was sufficiently self-reliant. Our son, then seven, was another matter. He was bright enough, but had been unable to perform well in school. Above all, he was a psychologically fragile, not adapted to knocking about in the Foreign Service. He and I had become especially close, so that the separation was bound to be difficult for him. Still, the tour was to be only eighteen months instead of the normal two years. And there was a provision for returning to the United States every six months for family visits. So I hoped that he too could survive, the more so as there seemed no alternative financially.

Explaining why Saigon was singularly suited to consolidating my Foreign Service formation will require a shift of gears from my account of parish ministry. I will need to describe the overall situation in Vietnam at the time and also the responsibilities of the office to which I was assigned. I will do so from the perspective of the American policymakers, first in the Kennedy and then in the Johnson administrations. This perspective was essentially a matter of the domino theory, the apprehension that the completion of communist control of Vietnam would be followed by a take-over of neighboring countries, not only Cambodia and Laos but also Thailand, Malaysia, even Indonesia. To be sure, the willingness from the United States to show force at that time may have been a factor in the thwarting by a knife-edge of a communist coup to take over Indonesia. Nevertheless, serious questions have been raised about the validity of this perspective, even within its own terms of reference. This was done latterly, and most impressively, by Robert McNamara, the Secretary of Defense in both administrations and leading proponent of the Vietnam War. His post-war conclusion was that the Viet Cong leadership was interested in national sovereignty not in regional hegemony; he said that except for profound mutual misunderstandings, some sort of deal might have been worked out. From a theological standpoint, a still further question might have been raised: should we suppose that we have to make history come out in a certain way? At the time, though, an alternative to the domino theory was difficult to envisage.

My previous Saigon posting had ended in late 1955. By that time, Ngo Dinh Diem, the President, had accomplished what a year previously would have seemed incredible. From the shakiest of starts, he had consolidated his hold not only in Saigon but also throughout South Vietnam. Diem was not only overcoming an entrenched non-communist opposition but also leaving no obvious space for the Viet Cong, to whom the northern half of Vietnam had been allocated. The next few years were marked by relative quiet, the Viet Cong being preoccupied with consolidating their hold on the North. In the early 1960s, however, they gradually resumed their activities in the South. Diem was aware of this threat and moved to counteract it. But coming out of the Vietnamese equivalent of the Chinese mandarin tradition, he relied on authoritarian methods rather than the mobilization of popular support. A feature of these was his portable guillotines, with which he disposed of numerous opponents actual and suspected. They were not without effect, but in the end they proved futile.

The fading of Diem's initial bright promise, and the consequent need to shore up his regime, did not go unperceived in Washington. The American response was at first confined to a few military advisers, but when these proved insufficient additional advisers were sent and then some combat troops. When these too failed to stem the Viet Cong advance, the American embassy, in particular the ambassador, turned on Diem in frustration, engineering a coup that resulted in not just his removal, but also his death. He was replaced as president by a series of generals, who were to prove ineffective in turn. The American build-up continued anyway, approaching its height about the time I arrived. It seemed that American power coupled with American resolve must prevail where the French, in their decades-long attempt to hold onto their colonial possession, had failed. For American power to be effective, though, a degree of economic stability would have to be maintained amid all the disruptions of war. The economic section, a joint embassy-USAID office, was charged with the responsibility for this, not just through monitoring prices and other economic indicators and co-ordinating monetary, fiscal, and exchange rate policies but also through assuring supplies of basic foodstuffs—rice, pork, and other rurally produced commodities—for the urban areas, particularly Saigon. Saigon, it might be noted, was situated on one side of the Mekong Delta, the provinces of which were the main sources of its food supplies. In the countryside Viet Cong, control was widespread, which added to the complexity of assuring these supplies. My assignment in Saigon was to the joint embassy-USAID office.

The atmosphere of this office was of the most intense. Though it had a director, the person effectively heading it was simultaneously Economic Counselor of Embassy and Associate Director for Program of the huge USAID mission. This was the Roy Wehrle whose major contribution to my own development I acknowledge in the Preface. He was thirty-three when I arrived and brilliant; for example, the following year, he won the William A. Jump Award, bestowed on the outstanding younger public servant in the entire United States government. In accordance with the critical nature of their responsibilities, he expected high performance from the members of this office. They had about a month after their arrival to prove themselves capable of it. Otherwise, they were shipped out regardless of the personal hardships that this might entail. I made the grade, despite my faltering performances in my previous postings and having been out of the government for a full four years. Had I failed to do so, the consequences would have been grave for me and for my family.

In my previous assignments, I had never been called on perform at such a level, nor do I think that I could even if I had been. What made the difference, I believe, was my seminary studies, particularly of the Bible and church history: the accounts of Israel's tenacity in the face of the opposition it encountered even in Canaan, the land that had been promised to it; the steadfastness of the early church's martyrs. These studies had infused an iron into my bones that previously they lacked. The story I am telling is concerned primarily with the contribution that Foreign Service and other secular disciplines can make to theology. But the flow can go also in the opposite direction; here was a case in which theology reinforced Foreign Service disciplines.

We worked sixty or more hours a week, striving to meet our continually arising deadlines. These were for, among other things, obtaining information for which a special need had arisen or completing reports on critical aspects of the economy. Generally our reporting took the form of memoranda to be circulated within the embassy or of cables to go back to Washington. At our staff meetings, usually chaired by the Economic Counselor/Program Director (Wehrle), we would be required to give accounts of what we were doing, so that not just he but all office members would be aware of it. At the same time, we would be given an account of the larger picture into which our assignments fit. As never before, I found myself being given assignments that I did not know I could carry out—or thought that I could not carry out—only to find that I could. As part of a team, I was being relied on implicitly to do so. I would not have been aware of holidays occurring at this time except for one thing. Marine guards were posted at the entrance to our building to protect it against terrorist attacks. On the holidays, they were more relaxed in the way they checked us in. Paradoxically it was through Wehrle, not himself a career Foreign Service Officer,

Theology and the Disciplines of the Foreign Service

that I was opened to the Foreign Service's core attributes: a willingness to face any challenge no matter how daunting, to accept any assignment no matter how difficult.

At the time, Vietnam was noteworthy for evidencing how one adapts to physical danger. Congressional interest in Vietnam was high, and we had frequent congressional visitors. I was designated the control officer for one of them, a senator from Iowa, making sure that all his requirements were met. Pursuant to this, I went one morning to pick him up from the apartment in which he was lodged, located in central Saigon. As I waited for him to finish dressing—he had been still in his underwear—some shots rang out further down the street. This was not unusual; I paid no particular attention. The senator, however, took it to be something serious, becoming angry with me for my lack of alarm. It was with some difficulty that I calmed him down. On another occasion, I was talking with a French official in a restaurant on the edge of town. We were on a veranda, overlooking the adjoining fields. Presently, an artillery battery began firing not very far away. Rather than stop our conversation, we simply raised our voices so that we could hear each other over the noise. We did this without quite realizing what we were doing. I was not completely inured to danger, however. Two or three days before my final departure from Vietnam, I was assigned to go on a helicopter tour of the southern coast, scenic but sparsely populated. We flew low just offshore, within easy range of any Viet Cong rifleman who happened to be about. Having made it this close to the end of my tour, I found myself quite anxious about making it the rest of the way.

Within my office the main function that fell to me was the monitoring of supplies coming into Saigon of pork, the most important foodstuff for the population after rice. Their volume had political and economic significance. The pigs originated in the provinces of the Mekong Delta, where the Viet Cong had widespread control and thus were in a position to limit their passage or, more typically, to levy taxes on it. Thus the numbers arriving in Saigon were an indication of the security or lack thereof in those areas. My task was facilitated by the fact that most of them went to the municipal slaughterhouse to be slaughtered. I had only to go there once or twice a week to collect the figures, which the slaughterhouse director, who became a good friend, readily gave me. Collecting them was not entirely simple, however. In the absence of refrigeration, slaughtering was performed early in the morning, before dawn, and the slaughterhouse was located at the far end of Saigon. This meant getting up very early myself. Usually, I went there on my bicycle, passing through the still-quiet streets in the dim dawn light. I made an exception to this, following a warning that an attack was planned on me as I pedalled along. Thus for a while I had an embassy car take me there. Eventually, though, I reverted to my previous mode.

There came a time when the price of pork rose sharply, giving rise to fears of economic and political instability. This occasioned my going beyond my monitoring function to develop a plan for a cold storage facility in Saigon. Frozen pork, whether domestically produced or imported, could be stockpiled there for release in periods of market dislocation either by the Viet Cong or by profit-seeking middlemen. My plan was welcomed both by Vietnamese officials with whom I was in contact and by interested Americans in Saigon and Washington. It was only partially implemented, however, to some extent because of bureaucratic complications that arose but also because supplies from the delta began to improve, possibly on account of the existence of an alternative to them.

Keeping tabs on economic developments in the provinces was also a function assigned to the office. As one of its members, I was required to make frequent field trips, over to the Mekong delta and up to central Vietnam as well. These involved going out to Tanh Son Nhut airport at gut-wrenchingly early hours to catch the small planes flying to provincial towns, operated ostensibly by Air America but actually by "a US government agency." The reason for going by plane was that most of the intervening countryside was too insecure to permit travel by road. I would spend a few days talking with knowledgeable people in these towns and in making sorties into the surrounding countryside. My fear was not so much of being shot at as of being captured by the Viet Cong, as one or two people associated with my office had been. I doubted that I could survive that ordeal.

It was on my return to Saigon from a trip to investigate rice supplies in a province to the north that I had the most hair-raising experience of my tour. The pilot of the plane remarked that he was running low on fuel and would have to land at Phan Thiet, a coastal fishing town a couple of hundred miles north of Saigon, to refuel. Presently he did so and pulled up at the airfield terminal. There was nobody to be seen, this in the midst of an active war zone. Had the base been overrun? Were the Viet Cong waiting to leap out and capture us? Finally, a single Vietnamese soldier emerged, sleepily rubbing his eyes, and with his assistance the pilot filled the plane's fuel tank. By that time, the sun was setting; sunset was a favorite time for the Viet Cong to attack. We taxied to the end of the runway, to the very outskirts of a

Theology and the Disciplines of the Foreign Service

village from which past Viet Cong attacks had come. Only then did we start our take-off run. Nobody shot at us; we emerged unscathed.

One may ask what was the significance of these activities of mine for theology, however notable from a Foreign Service standpoint. What was their equivalent, in Foreign Service terms, of policy relevance? I carried them on in a setting in which the stakes seemed to be high, omnipresent physical danger intensifying my sense of their importance. By them I was obliged to perform at the highest levels of which I was capable and, further, to take whatever risks, psychological as well as physical, were involved. These activities enhanced my ability to recognize the significance of theological issues, to see what was at stake—often the most vital aspects of human existence. This recognition prepared me to grapple with these issues with similar commitment, however difficult they were of comprehension or radical in their implications.

There was another significance, no less important. The data that I collected and the analyses that I made of them were not just to be kept to myself. Instead, they were to be reported, in the first instance to officials in the embassy but also back to Washington. In doing this, I was required to bring out their significance for US policy, and to do so clearly and coherently. Further, the reports that I wrote had to be such as to survive the scrutiny not only of my superiors in Saigon but also of the numerous officials back in Washington keenly concerned with Vietnam—up to and reportedly including President Johnson. Any unclear expressions, any flaws of reasoning, would be pounced on, immediately and emphatically. The exercise was a strenuous but invaluable discipline, preparing me to be no less scrupulous in the interpretation of biblical texts that I preached on and in the analysis of theological issues that I expounded in my teaching.

My final time in Saigon was no less notable for making up what was lacking in my formation in the church. A remarkable conjunction of circumstances allowed this to happen. In the ten years since I had last been there I had heard nothing of the congregation that as a lay reader I had then led. I thought that probably it had not survived. Thus I was no little surprised to find it not only existing but greatly enlarged, with a priest of its own in charge. It still met in the French Protestant Church building, but the service was no longer in the evening while the French congregation held theirs in the morning. Instead, it was in the morning while the French Protestants, who had dwindled considerably, had theirs in the evening. Attendance at the Sunday services approached a hundred, mostly American military with some civilians from the American and the British embassies together with a sprinkling of Vietnamese. The American ambassador, Henry Cabot Lodge, attended regularly as did other embassy officials, and the American commander, General Westmoreland came, as he explained to me, when he was able.

There was a drawback to these distinctions, however. As a large group mainly of Americans meeting at a regular time and place and including some of high rank, the congregation qualified as a prime terrorist target. In fact, it seemed an even more promising one than the American embassy and others that had already been struck. Further, no special security precautions appeared to have been taken—albeit the ambassador would barely pause to shake my hand as he stepped outside after the service, perhaps to avoid exposing me as well as himself to danger. But for some reason, psychological perhaps or political, an attack never came.

There was a further serendipity. The priest in charge was a graduate of the same seminary as I, having preceded me by three years. He welcomed me to assist him at the two Sunday morning services. One weekend each month he flew over to Cambodia to take the service for the Anglican congregation there, leaving me in charge. It was here in Saigon that I had my true formative experience of ordained ministry. The building lacked air-conditioning, naturally, and wearing vestments, even an alb, could be trying. The war was very much around us. Artillery and bombs dropped from B-52s with their characteristic rippling sound could often be heard during the services. The pulpit from which I preached had a compartment just below the level on which I stood. It would have been an ideal place for a Claymore mine, the charge of which is shaped so as to make the blast go in a particular direction. The Viet Cong were rather fond of employing them. Sometimes before the service I would inspect the compartment to see if there was anything in it but sometimes, considering that I had to rely on the Lord anyway, I did not.

Particularly significant was what I discovered from preaching in those circumstances. The Old Testament prophets—Amos, Isaiah, Jeremiah, and the rest—could be preached and could be heard in a way that they could not in the serenity and physical security of churches back in America. This prompted me to reflect: the background against which the prophets proclaimed their message must have been of much the same sort. Their background, already alluded to in chapter 3 on my experiences at seminary, deserves elaboration. Following the initial difficulties of establishing themselves in Canaan, the Promised Land, the Israelites had enjoyed sustained peace, security, and prosperity under David and Solomon his son as their kings. But then came their division into a northern and a southern kingdom, coinciding with the time when the threat from the regional superpowers, first Assyria and then Babylon, was beginning to take shape. Most of the people, however, averted their eyes from the impending catastrophe with its implication of powerlessness, preferring to suppose that somehow it would not come to pass and that they did not need to be concerned about it—just as we regularly turn aside from the catastrophes, national and personal, looming over us. But it did come to pass. Samaria, the capital of the northern kingdom, fell to the Assyrians in 722 BC and Jerusalem, the capital of the southern kingdom, to the Babylonians in 587 BC. Both conquerors carried off the people, or at least many of them. Those exiled in Babylon were allowed to return some seventy years later. Of those whom the Assyrians had taken not much was ever heard.

The prophetic books of the Old Testament, despite their magnificent imagery and their soaring poetry, are not easy to understand. What they are referring to or what thread connects their successive oracles is not readily evident. Thus one might suppose that their concern was simply to predict the future or, somewhat more profoundly, to emphasize the retribution necessarily following from the people's idolatry and immorality. But with the stripping away of our normal security by the circumstances of our Saigon services, it became possible for us to perceive the true function of the prophets. This was to break through the false assurance that the people of the time were allowing themselves, to bring home to them that it was not on their own resources but only on the Lord that they could rely. It was for this reason the prophets could be both preached and heard in Saigon in a way that they could not elsewhere.

This perception led to another and still deeper insight. The nation's catastrophe, as it impended as well as in its actuality, posed a profound crisis of meaning: was the Lord unwilling, unable even, to keep the covenant that at Sinai he had made with his people, the covenant which ever since had been the basis of their mutual relationship? The task of responding to this question, of overcoming this crisis, fell to the prophets. To them it was given to accept their human powerlessness and, having done so, to look squarely at what was going on around them. They were also given the ability to look within the people, to see their corruption, their disregard of social justice, their idolatry. It was on this basis that they came to understand that the people and not the Lord had fallen short. Their message was not welcome; it was, in fact, the last thing the people of the time wanted to hear. But by delivering it, they overcame the crisis of meaning and preserved the validity of the covenant, so that a framework was maintained into which the Messiah could come.

This insight turned out to be of special significance for me later on, as I will describe in chapter 8, but it had an immediate effect as well. In accordance with it, in one of my Saigon sermons I asserted that America's prevailing in the Vietnam War was unlikely to be either as quick or as easy as we had supposed. Just then, Ambassador Lodge's wife Emily, also in attendance, fainted so that he had to carry her out of the building. The tropical heat of Saigon could have been the main factor, but my assertion may also have played a part.

In going back to Saigon for another posting, I had taken serious personal and professional risks. I reaped no small rewards for doing so, however. My Foreign Service career was reinstituted and set to continue. Further, my ordained ministry was retrieved from the impasse into which in my Washington parish it had fallen and was opened to important new possibilities. And now, as the end of my Vietnam tour approached, I could look forward to another overseas assignment, probably less strenuous than Vietnam, and to a reunion with my family.

BISHOP'S VISIT: The Rt. Rev. Chu Ban It, Bishop of Singapore, visited the Anglican congregation in Saigon, over which he had jurisdiction, at Easter 1966. Here he is on the steps of the French Protestant Church after the service, with the bespectacled Priest-in-Charge, the Rev. Theodore H. Evans Jr., on his left and the author, attired for Sunday, on his right.

6

Congo Embassy and Church

My next assignment, after Vietnam, was to the Congo, where I was to spend three years. On the Foreign Service side, I was called upon to deal with broader issues than those which had confronted me in Vietnam. These contributed to my analytical skills and other Foreign Service disciplines still undergoing formation. On the theology side, it was these disciplines that enabled me to play a key role in history of the Anglican Church of the Congo. And in the course of doing so I came upon one of the great missionary stories of the twentieth century.

After a difficult and dangerous posting like Saigon and my creditable performance there, it might be thought that I would have been assigned to a post that if not more modernized would at least be more restful. However, my next assignment was Kinshasa, the capital of the former Belgian Congo, which in the official listing also qualified as "difficult and dangerous."

The Congo was the scene of Joseph Conrad's late nineteenth-century novel, *Heart of Darkness*. The title was apt, although the darkness was attributable not so much of the indigenous people as to the Belgian colonizers, in particular King Leopold II. In the wake of the explorations of central Africa by Henry Morton Stanley and others, he appropriated it as his personal possession and proceeded to exploit its rubber-producing potential with utter ruthlessness. Natives were pressed into service as latex gatherers. When they failed to meet their prescribed quotas they would have a hand cut off, a sanction enforced by locally recruited paramilitaries known as the *Force Publique*.

The international outcry over this and other atrocities obliged Leopold eventually to relinquish his sovereignty in favor of the Belgian state, of which he continued to be king even while king of the so-called Congo Free State. Thereafter, the worst abuses began to be rectified, although the obedience of the people was still enforced by beatings and other severe penalties. In the early twentieth century, as Belgian business interests invested heavily in the exploitation of the Congo's abundant mineral, agricultural, and other resources, the liberalizing trend continued. Infrastructure was developed and widespread education was instituted so as to provide a literate work force for the mines and plantations. Their education was limited, however, to the primary level. Further, the colonial authorities did almost nothing to develop governmental institutions, even local ones, so as to provide the Congolese with an experience of self-government. Not surprisingly, no viable political parties emerged. The existing groupings remained largely tribal.

In the latter 1950s, "winds of change" were blowing in Africa. Independence loomed for British and French colonies, to which in most cases it was granted in or about 1960. These winds were felt also in the Congo, causing stirrings among the previously docile population. The Belgians began to doubt their capacity to handle the new situation, and their doubting appears to have developed into a species of panic. Thus still without having made any significant provisions for self-government, in 1960 they too granted independence to their colony. The unpreparedness of the Congolese for it is epitomized in the number of university graduates among them—there were only nineteen.

The Belgians' haste, on top of their failure to make meaningful preparations for independence, was a recipe for disaster. Almost immediately on the departure of the colonial authorities, the Congo was wracked by conflict. There was an attempted secession of Katanga, the province producing the bulk of its mineral wealth, prompted by the *Union Minière* and other business interests hoping to hold onto their stakes there. The secession was thwarted in large part through the intervention, including military, of the United Nations. But in the process Dag Hammarskjold, the UN Secretary General at the time, lost his life. Then the Simba Rebellion, a nativist uprising, engulfed the country's whole northeast quadrant. Other uprisings were occurring during this time too. In the meantime, would-be leaders like Lumumba and Mulele had shown their inability to establish themselves.

The former was actively opposed by the United States on account of his communist sympathies; the latter, after becoming a Maoist, allied himself with the Simba Rebellion. The Cold War was in the background even in the Congo, remaining so for many years. The result was a breakdown of public order and of the economy.

In 1965 Mobutu, a general in the Congolese army such as it was—it was derived from the old *Force Publique*—seized power, assuming the presidency in a coup. Thereafter, things calmed down but there were still outbreaks of violence, notably the rebellions of mercenaries originally brought in to help re-establish order. The last of these was in the east, centering in the city of Bukavu. The tensions emanating from it, however, were producing riots in Kinshasa. This last rebellion broke out in May 1967, just as I was arriving with my wife and nine-year old son.

The three years I spent in the Congo were by no means prosperous and peaceful. Nevertheless they represented the country's best chance in the post-independence period to pull itself together and to start moving ahead. There were no major rebellions, and although roads and other infrastructure continued to crumble, the precipitous downward slide of the economy paused. Production of copper, the Congo's main mineral resource and export, began to revive and its international price was strong. These factors had given the International Monetary Fund (IMF) sufficient confidence to institute a stabilization program in the Congo. The program was predicated also on the expectation that Mobutu, despite his background, would prove a sufficiently reliable administrator. The IMF has extended programs of this sort to many countries, designed to help them get through difficult economic transitions and put their finances on a sound footing. Under its program the Congo, so long as it remained within specified economic and financial parameters, was to receive substantial funds for the furtherance of the stability necessary for economic development.

My position was in the joint embassy-USAID economic section, where I became one of three members under the section chief, a Foreign Service Officer. Within it, the responsibility for monitoring the stabilization program fell to me. The central element here was the government budget. To the extent to which expenditures could be kept within receipts, such factors as prices, the money supply, and the balance of payments would tend to stay in line too. Keeping track of the budget was not entirely easy. The presidency, meaning Mobutu, had its own account not subject to budgetary controls but still drawing on general revenues. He used it largely to shore up support by distributing largess around the country, rather in the style of an African chief. Naturally, the figures for it were not made publicly available. But through contacts that I developed at the Congo's central bank, I was able to ascertain them. My findings and my analyses of them were reported back to Washington for the information of the Congo Desk in the State Department and of other agencies interested in Congo developments. In addition, my work was used by the embassy and the economic assistance mission (USAID) in urging appropriate policies on the government. In the beginning the Congolese government stayed reasonably well on the path that the IMF had prescribed for it. In fact, in one year it achieved an actual, albeit small, budgetary surplus.

I did sufficiently well at monitoring the Congo's performance under the IMF stabilization program, along with reporting on other aspects of the economy, that as the normal two years of my tour were coming to an end, the USAID mission director pressed me to stay on for a third. After I left, however, the Congo lapsed from the parameters that the IMF had set for it. Mobutu, who changed the name of the country to the supposedly more authentic Zaire, pressed ahead with a program of "Zairianization" involving a government take-over of a number of enterprises, especially foreign-owned ones, and the introduction of other distortions into the economy. Additionally, the price of copper, the key support of the economic edifice, declined—albeit this did not keep Mobutu and his associates from amassing personal fortunes. Thus through mismanagement rather more than adverse circumstances, the country missed the window of opportunity for economic stability and development with which the IMF's program had presented it. But given the intractability of the country's problems, the outcome might not have been entirely different even if Mobutu had come close to fulfilling the IMF's expectations.

So much for my job in the embassy. However, the application of my Foreign Service disciplines in the Congo extended beyond that. In fact, they enabled me to play a significant role in the history of the Anglican Church. On arriving in Kinshasa, I had found there to be not only a strong Catholic church established under the auspices of the Belgians but also considerable numbers of Protestants: Methodists, Baptists, Presbyterians, and others. There was no Anglican worship, though. Presently, I started a small congregation, consisting mainly of Americans and other expatriates but with a few Congolese members. It went along well enough. Then a year or so later it came to me, I still do not know how, to wonder whether there might not be some other Anglicans in the country. Considering its size, equal to that of the United States east of the Mississippi River, and its extremely rudimentary communications, this seemed possible even though I had not seen or heard of any. In Kinshasa, I had become acquainted with a number of Protestant missionaries, several with considerable experience of the country. I asked them about the existence of other Anglicans. They said yes, there had been some, over on the eastern side along the border with Uganda. Whether these were still there they did not know. The only way to find out, then, was to go and see for myself.

This was no simple matter. On account of the expense and time away from work involved, I could not go on my own. Instead, I would have to get the embassy to send me. But they would not consider my actual purpose a suitable one. Then I hit on a solution. Through a Congolese acquaintance in Kinshasa I learned of a gold mine somewhat to the north of the eastern city of Bunia, operated by a Belgian company (of which there were considerable still in the Congo), *Les Mines d'Or de Kilomoto*. I proposed to the embassy that for the sake of rounding out our picture of the Congolese economy, I go and write a report on it. My proposal was accepted. I duly visited the gold mine, going down into it (but was rather relieved to get up out of it again). While in Bunia, I was able to confirm that there were still some Anglicans, in a remote hamlet called Boga some fifty miles to the south. But the road leading to it, like most in the Congo, had badly deteriorated since independence. Further, no buses or taxis ran on it. Thus I was unable to go there at that time. With only several months left in my tour, I was unlikely to get back to the eastern Congo again. Still, the timing of my trip in one respect proved providential. The plane I had been on in getting from Kinshasa to Bunia crashed two weeks later, killing all on board.

The matter would have ended there except for the mission director's extension of my Congo tour by a year and also for another unexpected development. Some months after my visit to Bunia, the Protestant Council, representing most of the non-Catholic churches in the Congo, met in Kinshasa. The American ambassador gave a reception for them and, knowing of the services I was conducting, invited me too. Also attending it was Bezaleri Ndahura, who at the time was the legal representative of the Boga Anglicans. He was then a layman but not many years later he became the first Congolese archbishop in the Anglican Communion. We did not know each other, but the chairman of the Protestant Council, a Congolese, was also present and knew us both. With a gleam in his eye, he introduced us. I told Bezaleri of my *visite manqué* and he urged me to try again. The Anglicans had a vehicle, he said, and they could pick me up in Bunia and take me there. Thus the stage was set for my visit to Boga, which I was finally able to make in the latter part of 1969.

Even then, the trip was not without hitches. I boarded the plane in Kinshasa, but before it could take off I was evicted from it, evidently to make room for some high official. The plane took off without me, but with my suitcase; such was the Congo. A week later, I tried again, this time making it to Bunia. Bezaleri and a couple of other Anglicans were on hand to meet me at the airport. To my surprise, my suitcase was there, too.

The Anglicans' vehicle, a Volkswagen minibus of the sort known as a *combi*, itself had a story. The Simba Rebellion, though centered in Kisangani to the northwest of Boga had engulfed the whole northeastern part of the country, as already noted. A high government official, Jean-Foster Manzikala, later provincial governor of Katanga, in fleeing the rebels had gone to Boga, where the Anglicans helped him across the Great Rift Valley and into Uganda. The rebels, who themselves arrived in Boga shortly after, in their fury began beating the Anglican Archdeacon, Festo Byakisaka, evidently intending to kill him. For some reason, however, they stopped short. The *combi* was Manzikala's reward for the Anglicans' assistance.

Though we started from Bunia in mid-afternoon, night had fallen by the time we arrived in Boga. But the road was visible for the first part of the way. Unpaved except at the beginning, it was indeed in bad condition, with great washouts requiring considerable skill for their circumvention, causing the fifty-mile journey to take fully five hours. In subsequent years it was to deteriorate even more; by 1996 the journey was taking eleven hours. I was given the guesthouse, a one-room circular structure. It had no electricity—there was none in Boga—and I went to bed promptly.

The absence of electricity was not the only distinctive of Boga, as was brought home to me the next morning. Mine was the only white face for nearly fifty miles around. Except for Bezaleri, the community's first university graduate, no one spoke either English or French. But he undertook to be my interpreter and guided me around the various features of Boga. Though it was only a hamlet with a few hundred inhabitants, it had a primary and a secondary school and a small clinic, serving a wider area. It had also a sizeable thatch-roofed church, with a drum rather than a bell to summon the worshipers. We duly visited classrooms in the schools. We went to see some outlying congregations as well, one of which consisted largely of pygmies. Throughout, Bezaleri explained to me the significance and the history of these things. Thanks to him, I was able to communicate with Archdeacon Byakisaka and other leaders of the community and to know their quality. On the Sunday I preached, through Bezaleri's interpretation, and participated in the administration of the communion. Although the liturgy was in Swahili, which I did not know, I was able to follow it reasonably well. The local tribal chief had a prominent place in the congregation; still, the church leaders were clearly in charge.

My visit lasted only three days and four nights, but I came away from Boga with strong impressions. One was the quality of its leaders, highly competent and fully in control. Another was the discipline, the dynamism even, of the community. Not only was its self-reliance evident, it seemed also to have a potential to reach out beyond itself, transferring its special spirit to others. I was the more impressed with these features because of their contrast with what I had seen elsewhere in the Congo, where by that time I had spent more than two years. I had come across reasonably effective entities there before, but Belgians had always run these. There were also those run by Congolese, but they were consistently ineffective. Here, however, was one run by Congolese and run very well.

I wrote a report on my visit; this is what the embassy expected of me and, further, it is what one does in the Foreign Service. It was well received by the embassy in Kinshasa and also back in Washington. I attached a supplement to bring out the potential for expansion that I saw in the Boga church. I envisaged it reaching out somewhat as the early church did from Jerusalem, spreading from Boga to the north and south and on to the west and accordingly deserving of support. I urged that now was the time to seize this opportunity, which otherwise might slip away. Together with this supplement, I sent my report to Anglican headquarters in New York, London, and Kampala, the Ugandan capital. It made an impression particularly on Erica Sabiti, the first African archbishop of the Church of Uganda, who was at the same time Bishop of Ruwenzori, the diocese to which Boga as an archdeaconry was attached. It proved to be the catalyst in the decision to appoint a bishop to reside in Boga, access to which from Uganda was difficult on account of the need to traverse the Great Rift Valley. With the removal of this obstacle and with its own bishop to lead it, the expansion of the Anglican church of the Congo began. It did, in fact, spread up and down the eastern side of the country and then over to the west, eventually reaching Kinshasa and even the Atlantic seaboard. And from a community of around 25,000 it has become a church with perhaps a half million members and nine dioceses. As such, it constitutes a separate province of the worldwide Anglican Communion, with its own archbishop. To be sure, this expansion has not been without growing pains. The people's poverty and low level of literacy coupled with the chaotic state of the country have greatly complicated the tasks of catechizing new members and training additional clergy. The outside assistance that it has attracted may have diminished its self-reliance, even while contributing means for its advancement. The long-lasting strife in the eastern Congo, where most of its congregations are still to be found, has hit it particularly hard. But in the face of all these things it has not lost heart but has continued to expand. On account of its distinctive circumstances and traditions, it has a unique contribution to make to Anglicanism and to the church universal, while also supplying an Anglican ethos to the Congo.

The most important of its distinctives is that it has been an African church since its inception. The missionary who brought the Anglican church to the Congo was not a European but an African himself. The discipline, dynamism, and self-reliance of the Boga community that so impressed me in the course of my visit are largely attributable to him.

His story goes back to the latter decades of the nineteenth century, when the British first came into Uganda and other parts of east Africa. It was a tumultuous time, with bitter fighting among factions seeking to maintain their footing in the new situation. Along with the British administrators came missionaries, particularly English Anglicans. Among their converts was a young soldier, Apolo Kivebulaya. As his faith deepened he turned aside from his soldiering and offered himself in the service of the church. His effectiveness soon became evident, leading to his being given a particularly difficult assignment. The border between Uganda on the east and the Congo on the west is now the Great Rift Valley. But at that time, a considerable area to the west of it was under British jurisdiction. The tribal chief at Boga, which was in that area, had heard of Christianity and, finding it interesting, asked for missionaries to be sent to him. Two went, both English, but on account of running into difficulties with the local people they did not last long. Rather than leave the few converts that they had made to fend for themselves, it was decided to send Apolo in their place.

So he made his way westward, terrified, as he looked across The Great Rift Valley, by what might lie on the far side. He proceeded anyway.

Things went well for Apolo in the beginning. He had come equipped to grow his own food, which earned him respect and independence from the local people; it was by stopping their donations of food that they had forced the English missionaries out. Before long, however, tensions arose. A man's adoption of Christianity meant his giving up the charms and witch doctor spells on which he had been accustomed to rely, and thus a radical break with his previous life. The number of Apolo's converts grew, but the chief, perceiving a threat to his own position in this, changed from a supporter to an opponent. Things came to a head with the accidental death of one of the chief's sisters, for which Apolo somehow was blamed. He came close to being killed by the chief's adherents. Apolo was taken off by the British authorities and held in prison in Uganda until his case could be disposed. He was, of course, acquitted. Despite this experience, though, he was willing to return to his converts in Boga. He stayed there, even after the Boga area shifted to Belgian jurisdiction, for the rest of his life.

Apolo was tireless in proclaiming the gospel not only in Boga but also to the surrounding tribes, among them a considerable group of pygmies. Doing so in the very primitive conditions prevailing involved undergoing great physical hardships, but these did not deter him. It was not, however, just his personal ministry for which he was remarkable. He selected a number of adolescents to live under his auspices so as to form them in accordance with Christian faith. These adolescents subsequently became the leaders of the community, the ones I was so impressed with when I encountered them on my visit in 1969. Apolo died in 1933. The fact that the community he brought into being still stood firm thirty-six years after his death is a convincing testimony to the solidity of his work. Nor did he envisage establishing this community as all that needed to be done. And in his death he made this manifest. He was buried in Boga; his grave is still there. Traditionally in that part of the world a man is buried with his head pointing back to the place he came from—Uganda, in Apolo's case. But he had directed that his should point instead to the west, as a sign of the work that remained to be accomplished in the Congo. The impression of the Boga community's potential for reaching beyond itself that I had arrived at well accorded with this.

On a personal note, I had a strong sense of Apolo as a still living presence in Boga. It was if he had gone away for a few weeks but would soon be back. I am not sure how this came to me. Perhaps it was through the extensive conversations I had with Bezaleri Ndahura, my guide and the future archbishop, as he took me around to see what was there. Perhaps it was it was also through my interactions with the community's leaders. However this may be, his living presence has remained with me to this day.

BOGA CLERGY AND CHURCH: As described in this chapter, in November 1969 the author traveled from Kinshasa, the capital of the Congo, to Boga on the east side of the country, on the edge of the Great Rift Valley. Though not much more than a hamlet, Boga was at the center of the Anglican Church in the Congo at the time. Here the author sits among the larger part of the Boga clergy. The thatch-roofed Boga church can be seen behind them.

APOLO KIVEBULAYA in 1930: He was the Ugandan missionary who came to Boga in 1996, bringing the Anglican Church with him. He spent the rest of his life in the Boga area, laying the foundation that subsequently enabled it to spread throughout the Congo. The clergy in the previous photo were formed by him in their adolescence. His character is evident in his face, as is shown by this photo (Source: *African Saint: The Story of Apolo Kivebulaya* by Anne Luck, SCM Press, London, 1963).

Before concluding the account of my Congo years I need to note one more circumstance. As they were coming to an end, an idea for a book dawned on me, the book that was to be titled *To Restore the Church: Radical Redemption History to Now*. As related in chapter 3, at seminary I had been struck by the affinity with biblical criticism and the biblical tradition of the thought patterns of secular professions and crafts, notably those of the Foreign Service. These patterns could be seen as enhancing the intelligibility of the history of the church as well. Through the writing of a book bringing out this affinity, I could share my discovery of it with others. But I had barely got started on this enterprise. Along with my wife and now two sons, the second born in the Congo, I was off to our next posting: Korea.

7
Korea, Laos, and Washington Termination

This chapter deals with the time from my arrival in Korea to the end of my Foreign Service career, which came about after several years spent back in Washington, where I had arrived by way of Laos. When I left the Congo my career prospects were good, and for a while in Korea they became even better. But then the sky began to cloud over increasingly, until the sun was obscured. Through developments in Korea, Laos, and Washington over which I had little control, I came to have no career at all. In Foreign Service terms this was catastrophic, beyond what might be imagined from the outside. But it did not, in fact, leave me to wander in futility. Instead I was led, in perhaps the only way I could have been, to an activity more enduringly rewarding than the Foreign Service. Although I did not become aware of it until later, I had already made a start on this activity.

Korean Sunshine and Clouds

Korea was a desirable place to be. It was desirable both for what it had to offer as a country and for the sophistication of the work I was given to do there. My performance was well viewed in the embassy. On the theological side, I gained insights, too, but these came indirectly, as by-products of my

Korea, Laos, and Washington Termination

embassy work, rather than through functioning in the church as I had done in Vietnam and the Congo. This was despite a strong Christian part in the country's history and presence among its people. The salient point about my assignment to Korea was that there my Foreign Service career began to unravel, despite my solid performance there as in Vietnam and the Congo. It was brought to an end by the course of my subsequent postings, in Laos and back in Washington. Had it not been so brought, though, the rest of this story probably would not have happened.

I had been in Korea once before. This was back in 1946 when I was a soldier in the Japanese Occupation. While serving in a malaria survey detachment in Kyoto I was sent over to Korea to collect some samples of their mosquitos for comparison. To get there, I went by a rickety train from Pusan on the southern end of the Korean Peninsula—where the ferry from Japan had landed me—to Seoul, the capital and largest city, near the boundary with the then Soviet-occupied north. With my assistant, I had spent a couple of weeks poking around the nearby villages and farms in quest of mosquitos and their larvae. Just over a year had elapsed since the Japanese surrender. Japan was still devastated by the war, as described in chapter 1. But Korea, which had been under Japanese occupation from 1910 until 1945, was worse off. There was less destruction of industry and infrastructure, but there had been much less to be destroyed. The poverty of the people was even more striking, and the chances of their condition ever improving seemed even more remote. This was before the devastation brought about by the Korean War. In their initial onrush, the North Koreans had got almost to Pusan in the south, and they had captured and been dislodged from Seoul twice, all with concomitant destruction.

In the twenty-four years between then and my return in 1970, the situation had vastly changed. There was still considerable poverty to be seen. But Seoul had been rebuilt and extended, and the traffic on its streets was heavy. The country's industrialization, focusing on exports, was at an early and still vulnerable stage. But already its fiscal and financial systems had developed considerable sophistication. Yet all this was a far cry from the economic powerhouse that Korea has now become.

Korea was a different animal from the Congo even then, and not just in stage of economic development. It had a temperate climate albeit a monsoonal one and thus hot and muggy in summer and bitter cold in winter. It had a recorded history stretching back nearly two millennia, largely reflecting its exposure to the cultural influences and political ambitions of both China and Japan. Some, though not all, of its ancient temples and monuments had survived; moreover, one could drive about and see these things. And its people were bustling, not just because of their climate and history but also because for many it was a necessity for survival. For me, the following epitomized the difference with the Congo: In the Congo, when we in our embassy capacity would invite Congolese people to a dinner or a reception, we would phone them a day or two ahead of the date to remind them of the invitation. In Korea, when Koreans would invite us to such things, they would similarly phone to remind us.

As for the geopolitical setting, unlike the case in Vietnam, there were no active hostilities; the Korean War had been over for nearly two decades. The tensions to which it had given rise were far from resolved, however. North and South still faced off across the demilitarized zone, some twenty miles north of Seoul. This meant that Seoul was in range of the North's artillery. The US stake in Korea remained large. There was, to begin with, the huge investment made in fighting the Korean War. There was also Korea's strategic geographic position between China and Japan. And finally there was the continuing presence of large American forces still stationed in the country. The house that I am my family occupied was in fact on an army post. The country's economic stability as well as its military strength was accordingly of critical importance to the United States. The embassy, in particular its economic section, was responsible for monitoring economic developments, for assessing their significance, and for discussing the Korean policies relating to them with the appropriate government officials.

As in Saigon and Kinshasa, my assignment was to the economic section, again a joint embassy-USAID one. Its pressures, though not as great as in Saigon, were by no means negligible. Within it, my main concern was with the central government budget, perhaps the key element in the maintenance of economic stability. Substantial excesses of expenditures over receipts would, by increasing the money supply, exert inflationary pressures. I found the budget with its special accounts to be highly convoluted, something like the grammatical constructions of the Korean language, but I succeeded in mastering it. Bank credit, which was also an important factor, was similarly within my purview. Some American banks had established branches in Korea, and on one occasion I negotiated on their behalf with the Korean government. In degree of sophistication, these matters went well beyond any that I had dealt with previously. Discovering that I could after all handle them was a source of confidence for me in tackling theological complexities later on.

My performance was viewed well in the embassy, and my efficiency report after my first year there was a good one. On the basis of it and of the performances that I had turned in in Vietnam and in the Congo, I thought that I was now on the way to a further promotion and, going on from there, could expect a modestly successful Foreign Service career. However, the end was not like that, as I have already said.

An intimation of it was not long in coming. When the annual promotion list appeared, following the completion of my first year, my name was not on it. This need not have been because I overvalued my performance. The number of economists promoted each year had been fluctuating, and that year there was only one on the list. Still, it was a setback. I needed to get over the hump and into the upper grades to be assured of career longevity, and now my chance of doing so had been at least delayed.

A more portentous development followed that one. Tensions arose between the director of the economic office, a highly capable though somewhat temperamental fellow, and the mission director, bureaucratically inclined and less talented, who likely felt overshadowed. The mission director's response was to "take down the empire" of the office director, as one of my office colleagues put it. This involved cutting back the office's staff. Perhaps on account of some remarks about the mission director that I had made to the ambassador supposedly in confidence, I was one of those so cut. Thus from Korea, I was to be transferred to Laos. This was actually against the regulations since I was not supposed to be sent back to Indochina so soon. The move would be no less disruptive for my family. We had found Korea a congenial place to live as well as to work and were looking forward to a second tour there. In the Congo our older son's school situation had been miserable. In Korea, his situation had improved but now he was about to lose that gain.

KOREAN PICNIC: The author's two sons, Matthew (*right*) and Nathan (*left*), take part in a family picnic in the Korean countryside not far from Seoul.

The sequel for my office director, Tom Olmsted, was more dramatic. After Korea, he was made director of the USAID mission in Cambodia, a step up but a tragic one. This was happening as the Vietnam War was drawing to its conclusion, leading to the collapse of the whole Indochina edifice that had so painfully been constructed. Much of Cambodia had already fallen to the Khmer Rouge, the communist-inspired insurgents who later carried out the genocide of the Killing Fields. And Phnom Penh, the capital, began to come under rocket attack. The strains of maintaining what remained of the position of the US-supported government were enormous. Olmsted was charged with finding riverboat captains in Saigon willing to take rice, the staple food, up the Mekong River to Phnom Penh so as to keep it supplied. This required running the gauntlet of Khmer Rouge fire from the river's very banks. On his last Saigon visit, he was unable to locate any such captain. And under this and other pressures and dangers he developed acute pancreatitis and died, as he probably would not have had he had access to treatment available in the United States. I was back in Washington at the time. His memorial service was in the Washington Cathedral, and it fell to me to conduct it. It was well attended by the upper ranks of the

Korea, Laos, and Washington Termination

State Department and USAID, who told me afterwards that they had been deeply impressed.

In Korea, however, I lost interest neither in the church nor in theology. Where the church was concerned, for a while I led a service in the Anglican cathedral in Seoul, mainly for expatriates, and I was in touch with Korean Anglican clergy. The arrival of the Anglican church in Korea was relatively recent, however, and it had not made contact with the people in the way that some other Protestant churches had, or in the way in which it has done elsewhere, notably in Africa, where its growth has been explosive. The Anglican Church of the Congo, about which I wrote in the previous chapter, provides only a minor example of this growth. Largely on this account, my church activities in Korea were not fruitful of theological insights the way that they had been in Vietnam and the Congo

Still my time in Korea was significant theologically. For in it I was able to make a start on the book, the idea for which had come to me as I was about to leave the Congo. Once settled in Korea, I found that I could, in fairly short order, sketch out the first six chapters. My aim was to convey the insights that I had gained at seminary concerning the biblical tradition and its communicability—these being the insights that I had deemed of prime importance for the church. (I gave an account of them in chapter 3, concerning my seminary experience.) I decided that my first chapter would deal with the Pentecost event in the light of the interpretation of it that I had happened on at that time. For as so interpreted, Pentecost reflects the communicability of the gospel in the ancient world. In this way it points to the potential for communicating it in our own time. The second chapter would set out the principles and methods of biblical criticism, which for me had unraveled so many of the difficulties that the Scriptures presented. The third would deal with biblical miracles, my greatest stumbling block in my early attempts to get into the Bible and its meaning. The fourth would go directly to Jesus' resurrection, the supreme miracle, without which the Christian faith is incoherent. The subjects of the fifth and sixth chapters would be, respectively, the Exodus and the prophetic movement, the two critical turning points in Old Testament history. In my account of the Exodus, I hoped to bring out the high drama of the event as well as its essential meaning: the establishment of a covenant relationship between the Lord and his people. For the prophetic movement, I would draw on the insight that had come to me not at seminary but during my subsequent Foreign Service tour in Vietnam, namely that it was through the prophets that the crisis of meaning provoked by the destruction of the nation and the exile of the people was overcome, that the validity of the covenant was maintained.

In dealing with the subjects of these chapters I would be drawing on my Foreign Service disciplines, employing them much as I would have in reporting on developments in countries where I was posted. I supposed that these chapters, together with some introductory material, would sufficiently establish the compatibility of modern thought patterns with the biblical tradition. Since the discovery of this compatibility had so fascinated me, I supposed it would not only fascinate others but also bring home to them the relevance of the church to the world in which they lived. In this way, it would contribute to the restoration of the church, as in the title *To Restore the Church*. As I was working out these chapters, though, I came to realize that showing this compatibility was not enough. To make the connection of the biblical tradition with our time fully convincing, I would need to show also how the church to which it had given rise had gone from the spiritual strength coupled with material weakness with which it began to the material strength coupled with spiritual weakness in which it now largely finds itself. In short, I would have to work out the *Radical Redemption History to Now* of the subtitle. And bridging a time span of this length would be a formidable undertaking. To be sure, I had some materials already at hand. For the bridge's abutment, as it were, in the early, pre-Constantinian church I had the A++ paper on its martyrs I had written at seminary. As a late medieval/early modern abutment I had my similarly written and acclaimed paper on Archbishop Cranmer (see chapter 3). But I had nothing for the time in between or for the modern period either. Thus the task would probably surpass anything I might hope to accomplish while overseas in the Foreign Service. Its accomplishment would therefore depend on more propitious circumstances arising in the future.

Before moving on from Korea, however, I should speak of the remarkable place that Christianity has achieved in that country. After all, the underlying concern of this book is with theology, and theology is intended to serve the church, in Korea as well as elsewhere. In my time there the main religious influences on the Korean people were still those of Buddhism and Confucianism, both emanating from China. But the number of Christians, already large, was increasing. As I write it is poised to overtake that of Buddhists, amounting to one-third of the population. The strength of Christianity was evident in the many church buildings to be seen in the cities. Indeed, Seoul had probably more than any other Asian city except Manila.

The work of foreign missionaries played an essential part in this, but it was not the whole story. The Japanese occupation, lasting from 1910 to 1945, was fiercely resented by the Koreans. As might be expected, the Japanese cracked down hard on any signs of revolt. But they hesitated to take such measures in the presence of foreign missionaries. Since these sympathized with the Korean cause, the dissidents could find some shelter behind them. Thus Christianity acquired a connection with Korean nationalism, which enhanced its appeal not only while the Japanese were present but also after they were gone.

A feature of Korean Christianity is the predominance of Calvinism in the churches, at least the Protestant ones. This is not the first time that nationalist movements, or emerging groups within restrictive structures, have found inspiration in it. The Netherlands under Spanish rule in the sixteenth century and English merchants hampered by feudal survivals, along with similarly encumbered French Huguenots in the seventeenth century, are further instances. The role of Calvinism in secular history will be elaborated in the next chapter. But the Koreans seem so far to provide the only Asian example of this role.

The essential point about Korean Christianity, though, is its demonstration of the power of the gospel. To be sure, this has not been apparent in modern times in the West as it has in Korea and no less in Africa. But it must exist there too, albeit latently. A central aim of this book is to bring this latency into the open.

Laos: Afflictions Professional and Familial

We now revert to my Foreign Service career and its unraveling. The story may not make for easy reading; my Foreign Service career was not without traumas. However, in joining the Foreign Service, one accepts that such outcomes—along with exposure to hardships and physical danger—come with the territory. This limits one's grounds for complaint.

The story picks up again in Laos, following my rather abrupt transfer from Korea. Laos is a moderate-sized but sparsely populated Southeast Asian country, across the Mekong River from Thailand and bordering on Vietnam, Cambodia, Burma, and China. Culturally, it falls on the Indo-side of the Indo-China divide, sharing with Cambodia as well as Thailand the Hinayana variety of Buddhism with its saffron-robed monks. There was and still is little industry, the economy being almost entirely agricultural.

Fighting was going on at the time, mainly between the US-supported Lao government with its tribal auxiliaries and the Viet Cong-allied Pathet Lao. But it was never on the scale of that in Vietnam or even Cambodia. In Vientiane, the sleepy capital, the conflict seemed far away. In fact, Vientiane made the Congo's Kinshasa seem bustling.

The Lao economy was not without interest, however. The dislocations of war meant that special efforts were required to maintain economic stability. This was done largely through a foreign exchange fund supplied by France, Britain, and United States. I was not involved in its administration, which was the province of another member of the economic office. The one other area of economic significance was the government budget. Somebody else, too, was assigned to this; I was left without much of importance to do. The office was staffed this time entirely by USAID Personnel instead of, as before, by those from the embassy as well. The director had a PhD in economics from Harvard. But instead of being helpful in his analysis of the economy and in his direction of the office, his Harvard training hindered his leadership. The mind-set it had given him was academic and a bit old-fashioned at that, rendering him not very capable of grasping the strategic implications of Lao economic developments. Things were not made any easier by the fact that the economic office, along with the rest of the USAID mission, was housed in a specially constructed building which, presumably on account of security concerns, was windowless. It was an oppressive place in which to work.

My lack of a significant assignment did not greatly damage my career, however, for I spent only about nine months in Laos. The full story of my family, were it to be told, would need to be told elsewhere. But I will note that Foreign Service life and its stresses can take a heavy toll of families. Family members inevitably play a part in a Foreign Service career, and it was for family reasons that my tour in Laos was foreshortened. Our older son scored high on aptitude tests, but at the same time was fragile physically and psychologically. This was not auspicious given the likelihood of his having to leave one foreign country and resettle in another every two years or so. Most likely, my separation from him while I was in Vietnam was decisive in exacerbating his psychological fragility—thus confirming my apprehensions for him at that time. As a result of these factors, and evidently a degree of dyslexia, in the Congo he had performed poorly in the only school available to us. In Korea, he had fared somewhat better. Still, we had misgivings about his prospects in Laos, in view of its remoteness and its paucity of educational facilities. An American neighbor of ours in Seoul had spoken highly of an American-headed boarding school in the Philippines, in the mountain town of Baguio, north of Manila. Despite the distance from Laos, it seemed a better bet for him than what he might encounter in Laos. So on our way to Laos from Korea, by way of home leave in America, we stopped in Manila, planning to take him the rest of the way to Baguio.

The beginning was not auspicious. We arrived in Manila in the midst of a weeklong typhoon, the rain causing some of the severest flooding ever to occur in the Philippines. Roads were impassable and nothing was flying. We were stuck on Manila. In the end, we had to leave our older son with an American embassy friend, to be sent on to Baguio when travel there again became possible, while we and our younger son continued to Laos.

Reportedly, he was doing all right in the Baguio school. I was able to visit him from Laos a few months later and his teachers were reassuring. But all was not well. Not long afterwards, he had what was diagnosed as an acute schizophrenic episode by a psychiatrist in the hospital at the American base of Clark Field, where he was taken for evaluation. That meant that we had to withdraw him from the school and bring him with us back to Laos. It meant also that shortly after, together with my family I was transferred to Washington, where treatment for him would be available. For the next several years, he underwent psychotherapeutic treatment. He was able to attend high school and to graduate although just barely. The longer-term effectiveness of his treatment turned out to be even more limited.

Washington End Game

Among the many questions facing me on my return to Washington was that of an assignment. These were not ordinarily available on such short notice. But the USAID mission director in Laos kindly found a position for me on the Laos Desk. I was able to remain there until after the collapse of the entire US position in Indochina in 1975. Much of the work was routine, as in preparing budget requests for submission to Congress. This time, however, instead of being excluded from the supervision of the Foreign Exchange Operations Fund, or FEOF, I was given responsibility for the Washington end of it. Thus from the standpoint of work I was better off than I had been in Laos. There was a succession of Desk Officers under whom I served—three altogether—and they viewed my performance variously.

In the collapse of 1975, Cambodia was first taken over by the Khmer Rouge, then Vietnam by the Viet Cong, and finally Laos by the Pathet Lao—similarly opposed to a government that the US supported. It had been thought that the Pathet Lao might be content to remain in the eastern part of the country, where they had mainly operated. But they took the occasion to move on the west and on Vientiane, confiscating not only US-government property but also personal possessions of the Americans still there before allowing them to leave—but I with my family had left already. This meant the end of any American presence in the Indochina countries. The Asia Bureau of USAID in Washington, which had committed many of its people to the region, accordingly underwent a major restructuring. The Laos Desk continued to function for some months thereafter, dealing with residuals. What fell to me mainly was to write a history of FEOF. This was scarcely the way to win promotion, but the time enabled me to continue, outside the framework of the office, the writing of my book. Were it not for that book, I would not be writing this one.

Within the office framework, I was able to pursue a special project. In Vietnam, I had become acquainted with the chief, a brilliant young Frenchman, of the International Monetary Fund mission that visited Saigon from time to time to check on the status of the Vietnamese economy—the standard IMF practice with its member countries. Back in Washington on the Laos Desk, I contacted him again. I was struck with how even after the 1975 collapse and the Viet Cong take-over, the IMF missions to Vietnam had continued. I began to talk with him about them. He reported that despite its communist orientation the new government was disposed to be pragmatic and desired relations with western countries, as well as with the Soviets and the Chinese. In our further conversations concerning his missions and their findings, it dawned on me that just as the United States had eventually re-established relations with China, in twenty years or so it would almost inevitably with Vietnam (diplomatic relations were in fact re-established in twenty years). This being the case, it would clearly be to the US advantage to begin the process now. The delay in re-establishing relations with China following the communist takeover there could be seen as having contributed to the Korean War and its intractability. Similar misfortunes might be averted by early action regarding Vietnam. In the reports that I submitted of my conversations with the IMF official I tried to promote this idea in both USAID and the State Department. These reports circulated

Korea, Laos, and Washington Termination

at surprisingly high levels but with little effect. It seemed that resentments from having lost the Vietnam War were still too strong.

The State Department some years before had established a dissent channel to enable lower-level officers to get views diverging from the official line to the Secretary of State or his associates, without being blocked by an ambassador or office director or some other intermediate official—there were notable instances where this had happened, with disastrous consequences. So I availed myself of it to reiterate my contention about post-war relations with Vietnam. Again, my initiative had no apparent effect, but at least it enabled me to feel that I had done what I could. And as described in the Prologue, it became the occasion for this book.

Eventually, the Laos Desk was also shut down and its people shifted elsewhere. The question arose of what to do with them. In my case, it was answered by a stint in an office still within the Asia Bureau but concerned mainly with producing surveys of peripheral countries like Burma, surveys not connected with particular developments but only with general issues. The stint did not last long, however. After a few months, I was shifted to a non-regional bureau entitled Programs and Policy Coordination (PPC). If I am a little vague about its functions, it is because I never really understood them. The office I was placed in produced studies of across the board economic issues rather than those related to particular developments or countries. As such, they involved working from statistics with mathematical models and thus a high degree of abstraction. Whether they would ever become relevant remained a question. Younger PhDs without overseas experience staffed the office. There were indications that I had been brought in because it was bureaucratically expedient for them. Needless to say, I was not comfortable there, nor was my supervisor approving of me. When the time came for my annual efficiency report, he panned me. This was a blow from which my Foreign Service career was not to recover.

This efficiency report coincided with an even more devastating turn of events; here, my family came back into play. On top of the already formidable strains imposed on it by my Foreign Service career had come those of coping with the mental illness of our older son. On account of them, though likely not only of them, my wife at this point decided to leave me, taking both our sons with her. I was then confronted not only with the isolation in which this left me but also with the problem of how to maintain at least some contact with our younger son, still only nine years old. I considered my relationship with him to be essential to his well-being; his mother, however, was disinclined to allow it. The upshot was a protracted and inevitably bitter custody contest, which in the end I lost. Thereafter, it was at most every other weekend that I was allowed to see him.

Nevertheless, I continued in USAID. Some improvement in my situation there came when I was transferred out of PPC to the Africa Bureau, to be Desk Officer for the small East African countries of Rwanda and Burundi. But my function in this position was the servicing of development projects, not the national economic analysis which I had focused on in the past. Thus I had little scope for performing as I had previously. Actually, during this time I received an offer that could have retrieved my Foreign Service career. The Laos Desk Officer whom I had favorably impressed subsequently became the Mission Director for Egypt, and on doing so he asked me to join him there. I declined because I felt I should not give up even the limited contact I had with my younger son. The Mission Director accepted my refusal with understanding.

My job situation turned decidedly for the better anyway. I was relieved of my responsibilities for development projects in Rwanda and Burundi and assigned to monitor the evolution of the Congolese economy, then at a potential turning point in its downward spiral. Not only was this the sort of analysis I was equipped to do, it was an occasion for contacts with the IMF and the World Bank such as I had enjoyed in the past. Despite previous disappointments with the Congo, the IMF was preparing to extend it a "shadow" stabilization program. This consisted in setting benchmarks for its budget, balance of payments, money supply, and the like to see if it could stay within them, before beginning the actual program. Quite unexpectedly, an IMF contact—not the one I had dealt with regarding Vietnam—phoned me to set out in detail how the program would work, leaving it to me to pass on this valuable information. I had just started to prepare a lengthy statement for the judge in my son's custody trial. I put that aside, though, to write a full report of the conversation with my IMF contact. Only after I had finished that did I return to the trial statement.

Integral to the IMF's project was a meeting of the Congo's main donors and creditors, the Belgians, the French, the British, the Dutch, and the Swiss as well as the United States, together with World Bank representatives and its own, to approve the planned stabilization program. This was to be held in Paris in December of that year. On account of my involvement with the Congo I was assigned to write the US position paper. This was generally regarded as a formidable task, to the results of which any of several

Korea, Laos, and Washington Termination

agencies—Treasury, the Federal Reserve, the Export-Import Bank among others—could take exception. My draft was adopted without dissent, and I was given a place on the US delegation to the Paris conference—the *Club de Paris*. Not incidentally, this enabled me on the way back to Washington to stop over in England and to spend Christmas with the first Anglican bishop to reside in the Congo, now retired. He, in fact, had been the missionary cited to me by the church leaders in Boga when I visited there in 1969. My report on my visit had been instrumental in his appointment to the position. Back in Washington, my performance continued to be appreciated, not just in my own USAID office but also on the State side. The State Congo Desk Officer, lacking my depth of background, looked to me for interpretation of economic developments reported from Kinshasa. When the time came, I was given a glowing efficiency report.

It came too late, however. Already in the previous summer, I had been notified that on account of low ranking by the promotion panel I had been designated for mandatory retirement. I then had two options: either leave quietly with nothing of the designation to appear in my record or else appeal it to the Foreign Service Grievance Board (an entity which had not existed at the time of my disgraceful treatment by my supervisor in Australia). For two reasons, I took advantage of the latter. Firstly, from the standpoint of the Foreign Service, which was still my standpoint, such an ending to a career was almost unthinkable. Further, I thought that surely my highly-rated service in "difficult and dangerous" posts, which Vietnam, the Congo, and Korea were officially reckoned to be, would allow me to prevail. On account of the Grievance Board's backlog of cases, mine did not come up until the following spring, allowing my participation in the Paris Club meeting already mentioned. Also in the interval, I was assigned to lead a mission to Somalia for an evaluation of the USAID program there, and for my performance on that I was commended. None of this, however, affected my designation; the bureaucratic wheels continued to grind. My case was taken up by the Board on my return from this mission, while I was still suffering from an intestinal parasite that I had picked up in Mogadishu.

The procedure was harrowing in the extreme. I could have engaged a lawyer but, considering that such a person would not sufficiently understand Foreign Service traditions, I undertook to represent myself (as I was doing already in my younger son's custody trial). Rather than concentrate on one or two factors in my favor, I presented a whole array, thinking that their cumulative weight would be sufficient—not an unreasonable expectation from a Foreign Service standpoint. At the hearing, I presented some witnesses as well as my own arguments, and I responded as well as I could to questions from the board members and to cross-examination by the "prosecution," a lawyer from the USAID Legal Bureau. The prosecution presented its own witnesses, notably the supervisors whose efficiency reports the promotion panel's determination was based on. The hearing went on for a couple of weeks. By the end of it, I was almost totally worn down. Back in my own office, where my performance had been viewed so favorably, I calculated my productivity to be only 25 percent of what it had been. But I expected it to revive and I awaited the outcome of the hearing with some confidence.

One afternoon several weeks later, I found the board's decision on my desk. It was a thick document examining all my grounds in turn. Instead of being cumulative in effect they were being made to stand individually, in accordance with legal principles rather than Foreign Service traditions. Rapidly leafing through the pages I found that one after another my contentions had been found insufficient. In the end, none were accepted. Thus the promotion panel's finding stood. I was to be given another month in my job, after which I would be terminated.

So my career would be ending in what was by Foreign Service standards disgrace. "Selection out," which this amounted to, was something that one did not normally speak about, much as used to be the case with cancer. There have been instances of suicide resulting from it. Personally speaking, having already lost one of the two main structures of my life, namely my family, I was about to lose the other—my professional career. The financial implications were also severe. Since I was eligible for an immediate pension, I would not be destitute. But my income would be only about a third of what it had been. Certainly I could no longer afford to take my younger son to restaurants and on outings, activities that had been the mainstays of my keeping in touch with him. But strangely, even in the midst of my shock and devastation, I had an intimation of deliverance, of being released for other and more meaningful pursuits.

This seemingly disastrous outcome actually turned out to be providential. I would not have left the Foreign Service on my own. The pay was too good and the work too interesting for that. Had I prevailed in the Grievance Board hearing, I probably would have continued in it until I was past the age—I was already in my latter fifties—when I could turn meaningfully to theology. The timing was providential in a very specific way as well, as I will relate in the next chapter.

There is an echo of this in T. S. Eliot's poem "East Coker," one of his *Four Quartets*:

> In order to arrive there,
> To arrive where you are, to get from where you are not,
> You must go by a way in which there is no ecstasy.

Or more simply, in explicitly Christian terms, it is necessary to pass through death in order to enter fully into life.

A final episode needs to be included to show the depth to which Foreign Service disciplines can become ingrained. It happened when my termination was only four days off. I had come down with a cold and I had a major dental problem. On top of these things, I was on the point of having to move out of the rooms I was living in—my wife had retained our house—and I had not yet found another place. In the Africa Bureau at that time a large increase in economic assistance to the Congo was under consideration. The Congolese Minister of Economic Affairs, who was in Washington, and the Congolese ambassador were scheduled to meet with the USAID Administrator in connection with it. As the concerned member of my office, I had already prepared the customary set of "talking points" for the use of the administrator, and I was to attend the meeting. Although it was not my responsibility to provide an interpreter (my own French was not adapted to the purpose), about an hour and a half ahead of the meeting I thought to check on whether this provision had been made; it had not. In the remaining time, I found an interpreter—a good one. At the meeting, the administrator made full use of my talking points; typically, high officials disregarded them as if to show their own familiarity with the issues. And he decided in favor of the proposed aid increase for the Congo.

I should add that even in the midst of all that beset me in Korea and after, I did not lose sight of my book—the project that turned out to be vitally important for me. As I have said, I now knew what remained to be done, namely to bring the story, the story of redemption history as I termed it, from the biblical period down to the present. I had some materials for doing this, albeit only a small part of what I would need. On these bases I made attempts to carry on with it, seeking the advice and support of some of my old professors at my seminary. I went so far as to submit drafts of what I came up with successively to several publishers. But these drafts, I am afraid, lacked real depth. This was not only because I was distracted by the goings on around me or because the research facilities I needed were unavailable to me. It was also because I was still not clear on how to connect the early church with the church of our own time. Thus not without reason—rejection slips can also be unreasonable—my drafts were successively returned. In the midst of this apparent futility, however, two things came about, both of prime importance.

First, I began to notice that the contours of the redemption history I was undertaking to trace down to the present somehow paralleled the contours of my own life. This discovery enabled me to discern a coherence in my life—a narrative within an overarching narrative of which I had never before been aware. In this discovery, to my surprise, I experienced release from the grip in which aspects of my devastating adolescent depression still held me. Thereby, I was also brought to the realization that redemption history is redemptive not just collectively or corporately but personally as well. In fact, in it probably lies the only true personal redemption. Although this idea perhaps seems bizarre, it turned out to have a substantial foundation, as will be described in chapter 9. Moreover, what applied to me should apply to the church as well: by becoming conscious of its own historical narrative it too would be restored. Hence, it was important to work out its history in the book.

The second came out of the succession of rejection slips itself. In the face of these rejections, I began to think seriously of giving up on the book. But just after receiving the last of the slips it came to me, as I was out jogging one morning, that the book had, after all, a unifying theme. Moreover, this theme could be expressed in a single sentence: *Power lies ultimately in acceptance of our powerlessness.* This is to say that our human power is essentially powerless and that only in our acceptance of our powerlessness is there space for God's power, the only true power, to come upon us. I saw that herein lay the unity of the three pivotal moments that I had discerned biblical history: the Exodus, the prophetic movement, and crucially the death and resurrection of Jesus. For in all three can be seen both this acceptance of human powerlessness and this inflow of divine power in the wake of it, as in the account of the book's first six chapters above. In this theme, I found also the key to subsequent history, secular as well as ecclesiastical, in which spiritual, not material, power is to be seen as ultimately prevailing. A major significance of this unity then dawned on me. Biblical redemption history, although it can never be replaced, can still be extended, so that it

Korea, Laos, and Washington Termination

may be seen as applying not just to the biblical period but also to our own time. To my knowledge, no such extension—at least no comprehensive one—had been undertaken before.

What I would need to do now was to fill in the outlines of post-biblical history made traceable by this theme. This would be a formidable undertaking, however, and in the bleakness of my prospects following my mandatory retirement, there was no assurance that an opportunity for it would present itself. But in fact one did, probably the only truly suitable one, as I will relate in the next chapter.

8

Properly into Theology

THE PROSPECTS FOR A way onward from the Foreign Service were distinctly murky, overhung as they were by the futility arising from my mandatory retirement. A further complication was the short notice that I had of it. Normally, those in the Service can anticipate their retirement by a year or two, allowing them leeway to make plans. I had only a month. But an idea came to me even in that time, a turn of events that I can only regard as providential. It was to go to work in earnest on the book that I had conceived of in the Congo. I had continued to be convinced of the project's importance. As already described, I had made a beginning on it in Korea and had extended it in some degree back in Washington. But in the midst of the distractions of both places I had not found much traction. Now, I could devote nearly full time to the project. At the last minute, I found a place to move to, solving the problem of where to live. Logistical difficulties remained, however. My new apartment was noisy and cramped, ill suited for writing. My access from there to libraries, advisors, and other supports that I would need was very limited. I still did not know whether I could get by on my drastically reduced income.

Here again an answer came into my mind, prompted largely by my having stopped off in England on my way back to Washington from the Paris Club meeting in late December 1983, as related in the previous chapter. I had done this so as to spend that Christmas with the Bishop of Boga, now retired there, and his family—he was the missionary whom the people of Boga had spoken warmly of during my 1969 visit. My visit with him reinforced my impression of England as a congenial place to be. Knowing of its ancient universities I thought that in one of them I should be able to work effectively on my book. I lacked UK connections, of course, and had little idea of how things operated there. I was fuzzy on even the country's geography. But the bishop, a graduate of Cambridge University, now lived in that city. So in him I might have a contact able to help. There was still the separation that my move would entail from my younger son, who was at the time only fourteen, and from my older son, too, albeit he was already twenty-four. In my last years in the Foreign Service I had been unwilling to accept an overseas assignment for fear of losing this contact. But this consideration was now less relevant. For one thing, I could no longer afford to take the younger one to restaurants and on outings, which had been our mainstay. For another, my attempts to maintain such visiting time as I was authorized had led to tension with his mother. Persisting in them would be likely to exacerbate it and thus be to his detriment rather than his benefit.

Within a month of my mandatory retirement I made an exploratory trip to England, looking at the universities of Durham, Cambridge, and Oxford, particularly the theological colleges (seminaries) associated with them. Of these, Ridley Hall in Cambridge seemed the best prospect, the retired Bishop of Boga having had his training for ordination there. Indeed it was through him that I was accepted as a visiting scholar for their winter term, to work on my book.

My arrival at Ridley with two heavily packed bags on an early January morning portended what I was to encounter. At first, I could not find a way in. Snow was on the ground, and the little wheels on my suitcases made tracks in it as I searched for one. The college at that time was without central heating. The rooms, including the one assigned to me, were heated by gas fires, which could not be left on overnight for fear of asphyxiation. It was a cold winter, and room temperatures would go down by morning to about freezing. For the sixty-plus residents in the college, there were only two washing machines and no dryer. Competition for line space in the "drying room" was heavy. The food was wretched. I theorized that conditions like this, which seemed to prevail in the university, had been considered a necessary toughening for service in the Empire. Before long I came down with a flu from which I did not recover for a month. The root of one of my teeth cracked, requiring it to be extracted. The British dentist I went to pulled the wrong one the first time around. Along with these hardships, I was undergoing effectively total immersion in British culture. Whatever one may have supposed about its affinities with American culture, on the spot one finds marked disparities. However, despite my foreignness and my being a generation older than most of them, the students, who as ordinands were preparing for ministry in the Church of England, treated me as one of their own. The faculty dealt kindly with me too. And Cambridge with its university held no small attraction. These aspects of my time contributed importantly to my ability to persevere.

During the winter term, I made a start at comprehending not only English ways but also how to avail myself of the resources of the university: its vast library, its excellent lectures, the willingness of eminent professors to talk with even an unlikely foreigner like me. I embarked on some of the reading that I would need to do for my book. A professor whose specialty was Reformation history guided me in that, allowing me to come to him for weekly discussions. I cannot say that he was very helpful; he did not really understand what I had in mind for my book. He did, however, contribute something important. When I inquired about sources for Luther's theology, he told me of a book that had just come out. Its author was young and previously unpublished, but it had been favorably reviewed, even in Germany. It was *Luther's Theology of the Cross*. His name was Alister McGrath.

As the term drew to an end I realized that I needed to stay longer in England if I was to accomplish anything substantial. I inquired about the possibility of doing so at Ridley only to discover that for the next term no room was available. From the students there I had heard of Wycliffe Hall, a comparable theological college in Oxford. I applied and found that they would take me in, albeit with some juggling of rooms for the first weeks. Thus I came to "the city of the dreaming spires." Although Wycliffe, like Ridley, enjoyed the distinction of being in the midst of one of the world's top universities, it presented many of the same difficulties. To be sure, the rooms there were centrally heated. But the food was little better, and as at Ridley I needed to fit in with a student body which, however welcoming, was of a different generation and culture with no comprehension of my previous life or profession. But having lost both career and family, I was starting over anyway.

Despite these difficulties, Wycliffe turned out to be the one place where I could be properly launched on my book. This was mainly because of the presence there of the above-mentioned Alister McGrath as a recently arrived member of the faculty. If ever I have met a certifiable genius, it is he. Stories circulated about him: how even while doing post-doctoral research in molecular biophysics at Oxford he had completed his theological studies, receiving first class honors in them; how with his photographic memory he needed merely to glance at a page in order to comprehend it. I once asked him how he kept track of the hundreds of footnotes in his scholarly books. He answered simply, "In my head." Not only could I profit from the extraordinary clarity of his lectures, from his equally extraordinary energies I was able to pick up something of what my own lacked. His early promise was to be abundantly fulfilled. He had authored or edited more than fifty books by the time he was fifty. Not long after, he was chosen as the 2009 Gifford Lecturer, tantamount to a Nobel Prize in theology. The Gifford Lectures, for those who may not know, are a series founded by the Scottish Lord Gifford over a century and a half ago and are delivered in rotation in one of the four universities of Scotland. Lord Gifford's intention for them was to further a rational understanding of theology. All the eminent theologians, German- and English-speaking, of the twentieth century were Gifford Lecturers. On top of being distinguished in this way, McGrath has become probably the best-known theologian in Britain.

These considerations only sharpen the question of why he undertook to mentor me in my writing—not only in the beginning, but also through the additional decade I required to complete my book. I was not an academic; I had no advanced degree in theology. Instead of being some promising young fellow that he might have wanted to take under his wing, I was twenty-six years his senior. In fact, my only asset was my Foreign Service career—but it sufficed. Its sufficiency is further evidenced by our continuing correspondence. A few years ago, after not getting a response to a message that I had sent him, I wrote again to ask if he had received it. He answered, "I am always interested in what you have to say." The timing of my arrival at Wycliffe, before the pressures on him had acquired their later intensity, was a necessary condition, as already mentioned, for his taking me on. More of his story needs to be told, though, if his readiness is to be fully understood.

Growing up in a country town in Northern Ireland, he came to attention through his proficiency in his studies, particularly the natural sciences. On completing his secondary education he was given a scholarship to pursue them at Oxford. An outstanding career as a scientist no doubt awaited him. While studying at Oxford, though, he was converted from the atheism he had previously professed to Christian faith—he has said he does not know quite how. Following on that he turned his attention to theology, completing his theological studies with first-class honors as previously noted. In the earlier stages of his theological career his focus was on historical theology as that subject is termed, in particular on the Reformation and the Reformers themselves. I have already mentioned his Luther biography. Despite the massive amounts already written about the initiator of the Reformation, in both English and German, he came up with an account that was fresh and compelling. That he should have done so is no small marvel. He wrote a similarly notable biography of Calvin, enabling its readers to have a clear grasp of the Reformer's overall contribution as well as of the developments through which he arrived at it. The doctrine of justification was of central importance in the Reformation. McGrath produced a study of it not only in that context but also in its antecedents in the early church and in the Middle Ages. His investigations extended beyond this to the development of doctrine in general. Moving forward from there, he wrote impressive biographies of the contemporary theologians J. I. Packer and T. F. Torrance. Along the way, he became known for the authority and clarity of his theological textbooks, now translated into twenty languages. Nor have his works been confined to the academic, his *In the Beginning: The Story of the King James Bible* being among the many designed for a general readership. His fresh and incisive grasp of the issues and his extraordinary ability to convey them succinctly and intelligibly surely reflect his belief in their importance, as also in the importance of making them known.

The foregoing were largely expositions and interpretations, marked by unusual lucidity and accessibility, of the thought of others. Around 2000, however, his writing took a distinctive and original turn. This was towards the relationship between theology and the natural sciences, his early interest. He had not forgotten them and their disciplines. On the contrary, all along he had been struck by the correlations he saw between them and theology and was intent on giving an account of these. He understood that he needed to become thoroughly grounded in theology before embarking on it—so he waited twenty years to begin. He developed his new direction in several books, notably among them his three-volume *Scientific Theology* series. Its culmination though not its end-point may be seen in his 2009 Gifford Lectures, featuring Darwinian evolution and big-bang cosmology. His *A Fine-Tuned Universe? The Quest for God in Science and Theology* presented his Gifford thoughts in book form.

Out of his work has come a revised and newly relevant concept of natural theology. As discussed in the Prologue, this is the branch of theology which deals with the relation between nature (broadly conceived of) and revelation—a relation which, whether we like it or not, is determinative of how we view the world and our lives in it. In the early modern period, there were considered to be two sources, two books as it were, in which the character and purposes of God could be read, namely biblical revelation and nature. Their authority was considered more or less equal. This view, though, left unanswered the question of the relation between revelation as contained in the Bible and nature as constituted by extra-biblical observation. The question acquired urgency when serious conflicts developed between the two, particularly in the wake of Darwin's theory of evolution. The tendency was to resolve it through the interpretation of revelation in the light of the supposedly more assured conclusions of the sciences, including not just the natural but also the social. In this way, revelation became relegated to a secondary position, particularly in the latter nineteenth century. Effectively, it was subordinated to the prevailing humanly-derived culture and thus to merely human conceptions. In the first part of the twentieth century, however, there was a reaction to this relegation, in which it was seen not only as having eviscerated the gospel's ability to speak to the world but also, in its exaltation of the human over the divine, as having left open the way to the world wars and other catastrophes of that era. This reaction, associated particularly with the Swiss theologian Karl Barth, took the form of affirming the primacy of biblical revelation and its God over all else, an affirmation requiring in that context no small daring. But salutary as it was, it ran the risk of denying the character of the extra-biblical dimensions constituting nature as also part of God's creation.

McGrath's contribution here, as set forth initially in his *Scientific Theology* series, was to recognize a legitimate role for the natural sciences within the framework of revelation, that is, not as determinative of revelation but rather as casting light on its implications by their insights and methods. In this way he avoided the subordination of theology to them while still allowing them to contribute to it. Hence his *ancilla theologiae* or handmaid of theology concept, by which he designated this function. This was very much the function that I saw the disciplines of the Foreign Service as performing. By elaborating their nature and significance, I hope in some measure to be advancing his concept.

More immediately, herein would be a key to McGrath's willingness to supervise me in the writing of my book. To be sure, he had not yet articulated the ideas that I see as paralleling my own, nor had I yet made mine explicit. But he may have already sensed an affinity between them—we both had footings not only in academia and the church but also in the secular world.

McGrath supervised me largely by reviewing the sections of my book as I produced them. He did not give me a great deal by way of comments on them; however, the knowledge that someone of that caliber would be reading them already constrained me to my best efforts. Without the role that he played, I probably would have been unable to carry the book through to completion. And on its completion depended my further movement into theology, the subject of the next chapter.

Oxford itself played an important part in the process. Similarly to Cambridge, I had access to the university library, in this case the Bodleian, to lectures, and to eminent professors willing to talk with me about the aspects of their specializations that I needed to understand. I depended on them to point me to the relevant source materials. In contrast to the situation in my overseas posts and in Washington, where such work on the book as I had done had been in isolation, most everybody in Oxford was writing something. In this, I found significant reinforcement.

Even with the special advantages of Oxford, plus the considerable thought that I had already given to the book, I had difficulty getting started on what remained to be done. In fact, I began to wonder whether I would find the proper place to begin. My flagging confidence was restored in an unexpected way. I happened to visit another theological college, this one over in Bristol. While I was there, the college's principal gave me some time to speak with him. I took the opportunity to tell him what I had in mind for my book. Not only did he listen attentively, he conveyed to me his belief that it could and should be written. He was George Carey, later a Church of England bishop and then Archbishop of Canterbury from 1992 to 2002.

Some months later, my breakthrough came. Not surprisingly, it came in the writing of my section on Luther, the subject of McGrath's first book. His account, along with some others, provided me with the background that I needed. Figuring in it was the *anfechtung*, the profound spiritual unease that Luther developed once he became a monk. I was struck by its resemblance to the acute psychological distress I had experienced in my adolescence, which I spoke of in chapter 1. Particularly helpful for me was McGrath's story of how Luther's theological breakthrough finally brought him the release from his *anfechtung* that he had been seeking. Out of this breakthrough came first, the 95 theses which he posted on the door of the castle church in Wittenberg in 1517; second, the popular following which these attracted; third, the opposition of church and empire which this brought down upon him; finally, his affirmation of his convictions in the face of all the spiritual and temporal authorities convened to judge him at the Diet of Worms: "Here I stand; I cannot do otherwise; God help me." With this, the Reformation began.

Thereafter, my analysis no longer followed that of McGrath's or of any other Luther biography that I was aware of. Instead it came out of my experience of the Foreign Service as institution and establishment. Already at seminary this experience had enabled me to grasp that without its ability to stand over against the Roman state the early church would have been bereft of its spiritual power. Indeed when subsequently, as engineered by the Emperor Constantine, it was drawn into the state's orbit, it lost its much of its spiritual power. In the wake of the Diet of Worms, Luther allowed himself to come under the protection of the Elector of Saxony, his sovereign and sympathizer. Had he not done so, the religious establishment likely would have eliminated him. At the same time, his move allied him with the temporal authorities, the outcome being their substantial control of the church movement that he had inspired. While fully recognizing the magnitude of Luther's theological and ecclesiastical achievement, I saw this as the Reformation's basic flaw. My view was given substance, I believed, by Luther's response to the Peasants' Revolt of 1525, in which the German peasantry, direly oppressed by their overlords, rose up against them. They looked to Luther for support but, constrained by his temporal involvement no less than his doctrine of the separate realms of church and state, he condemned them, even calling for their extermination. Their suppression might seem to have been necessary for the maintenance of civil order of the time. But through its conservation of an antiquated economic and political status quo, it could also be seen as contributing to the Thirty Years War of the first part of the seventeenth century, which devastated Germany. This conflict, through its assumption of a religious guise and its consequent pitting of Protestants against Catholics, contributed substantially to the subsequent decline of religious faith.

From Luther, I found it relatively easy to move on to two other great Reformers: Zwingli and Calvin. It was Zwingli who, almost contemporaneously with Luther in Germany, brought the Reformation to Switzerland. Its presence there, as well as in Germany, contributed importantly to its survival. But Zwingli himself became involved with temporal authority—in his case with the Zurich city council—leading not only to a weakening of his reforms but also to his incongruous death in battle. Calvin, coming along a generation later and establishing himself in French-speaking Geneva rather than his native France, brilliantly organized Reformation doctrine in his *Institutes of the Christian Religion.* At the same time, he devised a system of church government not dependent on either bishops or state supervision. Calvinism played a major role not only ecclesiastically but also economically, politically, and socially in the impetus it gave to the modernization of Europe (as noted in my chapter 7 account of Christianity in Korea). Calvin did not entirely avoid entanglement with the state, constituted in his case by the Geneva council. But for him, this took the form more of drawing the state into the church than of the church into the state.

In my Reformation chapter, I did not fail to give an account of the reaction against the close church-state connection prevailing in the so-called mainline Reformation. This was embodied in the Anabaptist movement, also known as the Radical Reformation. In its representation of the marginalized, in its stand against those repressing them spiritually as well as physically, in its members' willingness to undergo martyrdom, it was evocative of the early church, prior to the toleration and official support accorded it by the Emperor Constantine (with consequent diminution of its spiritual power). In my research, I was astonished to find how closely the Anabaptist view of the pre-Constantinian church accorded with mine as described in chapter 3, on my time at seminary. Somehow, though, the Anabaptist movement seemed to lack the coherence of the early church and thus its staying power.

I prefaced my chapter by relating how the revival of commerce and industry in Renaissance Italy fostered habits of analytical and critical thinking in those who led it. These habits, the basis of Renaissance humanism, led to critical examination of the classics of the ancient world, aimed at establishing accurate versions of their texts. This examination eventually included the Bible. Out of it and of the extension of humanism to northern Europe came the reliable Greek text of the New Testament produced by the Dutch scholar Erasmus. It revealed the errors and distortions that had crept into the prevailing Latin version over the centuries. It had a major impact on all the main Reformers, thus playing a key role in the inception of the Reformation. I could not help being impressed by the parallel between the commercial disciplines arising in the Renaissance and those developed by the Foreign Service—both possessing the capacity to serve as theology's handmaids, its *ancillae theologiae*.

Having accomplished a rendering of the Reformation, I could then turn to the elaboration of the account that I had already produced of the pre-Constantinian church (see chapter 3). It was in doing so that I came up with my analysis of how Rome became Rome, how it developed disciplines and efficiencies rather like those of the Foreign Service. In accounting for the church's phenomenal spread despite Roman determination to wipe it out, I arrived at a transposition of the principle that I had discerned in biblical redemption history: "power lies ultimately in acceptance of our powerlessness," the power here being God's which, rather than the human, is the only true power. Now it became "when the church lacks material power it tends to be powerful spiritually; when it becomes powerful materially it loses spiritual power." The coincidence of the church's rapid spread through the ancient world with its strict adherence to non-violence accorded with the first part of this principle. So, too, did the key role that I ascribed to its martyrs in its eventual triumph over the Roman state. The second part of it can be seen as applying the to church's loss of spiritual power once the Emperor Constantine had drawn it into the imperial system. Constantine's conversion to Christianity is usually regarded a decisive advance for the church. But in line with my Foreign Service formation, I saw his main concern as the acquisition and retention of temporal power, at which he was brilliant, and thus his influence as a decidedly mixed blessing.

What confronted me, then, was the gap in time between the early church and the Reformation, consisting of the Dark and Middle Ages. My transposed principle of biblical redemption history availed me in bridging it. With the collapse of the Roman Empire and the breakdown of civil order in the West, the church regained substantial spiritual power. Indeed, as the one institution conserving a measure of stability amid the chaos, it provided a center around which a new order could cohere. Towards the end of the first millennium, it faltered as secular interests again obtruded, particularly on the papacy. In the eleventh century, though, the papacy underwent an extraordinary revival, substantially freeing itself from their control. In so doing, however, it was led to assert control over the temporal powers, leading to the monumental struggle between papacy and empire, now the Holy Roman Empire, which characterized much of the Middle Ages. In this struggle, the papacy prevailed for a considerable time. Its dominance led it, however, into two fundamental errors. These were the Crusades and the Inquisition, both of them diametrically opposed to the stance of the pre-Constantinian church. There ensued the decadence of the Renaissance papacy—moral and theological—which set the stage for the Reformation.

What now remained was to account for the post-Reformation, modern period. Conventionally, this is viewed as one in which the influence of the church receded, vitiated as it was by the Thirty Years War in Germany and prolonged struggles elsewhere, which however political in their basis, had taken on a religious cast. In the wake of its recession, the Enlightenment values of rationalism and individual autonomy came to the fore. My telling of the story recognized these Enlightenment values and their positive aspects, although I may have failed to accord them their full intellectual, social, and religious significance. But in the conventional version an element of no less importance is left out of account. This is the ascendancy of the modern nation-state. As led by my Foreign Service formation, I put my emphasis on it. It had its inception in seventeenth-century England, where the Calvinist-inspired mercantile class managed to throw off many medieval constraints including, during the period of the Commonwealth, the monarchy itself. From its ascendancy and that of its mercantile supporters stemmed the modernization of English economic and political institutions. From this, the Enlightenment itself took its rise. In the eighteenth century, Enlightenment ideas spread to France, contributing to the French Revolution and the emergence of a modern nation-state there. Portentously, that revolution was accompanied by full-blown nationalism, a phenomenon not previously encountered at least in that form. Germany's turn came in the nineteenth century, largely in reaction to Napoleon's hegemony. As a modern nation-state took shape there, it brought about the unification of the country and its formidable economic and military development.

In its modern form, the state was marked not only by its unprecedented efficiency but also by its emotional appeal, expressed in the nationalism stemming from revolutionary France. It could thus provide the collective identity which modern individuals, for all their supposed autonomy, still found essential. In this respect, it assumed a role formerly played by the church; nationalism effectively became the new religion albeit not generally recognized as such. Gathering force in the latter nineteenth and early twentieth centuries, it reached its apogee in Nazi Germany. The two World Wars and the Holocaust measure the cost of this idolatry—which the church, albeit with a few notable exceptions, failed to oppose.

Properly into Theology

In the post-World War II period I saw nationalism as losing much of its appeal. But as I noted, to the extent that it has it has left a void. What might come along attempting to fill this void, and the church's response to it this time, therefore remained to be seen.

I did not end the book quite there. Instead, in an Epilogue I told the story of Archbishop Cranmer which, along with that of the early church's martyrs, had struck me powerfully at seminary (chapter 3). In his evident personal weakness, in the stifling of his talents by the very institution, the Tudor monarchy, which had called them forth, and in his transcendence finally of these limitations, I found his life to be an apt summing of the history, personal as well as collective, which in the book I sought to convey.

I should add a methodological note on the application of the disciplines of the Foreign Service and other crafts to history and theology. As I proceeded with the book, I seldom had the luxury of knowing much beforehand about the periods I was writing on, spanning as they did two millennia of history. Therefore, I had to acquire a sufficient knowledge of each as I went along. Regularly, I went through a season of despair at the magnitude of this task, before managing to accomplish it. The procedure I arrived at was in fact one that I had already developed in the Foreign Service. It was to approach each historical period as I would have a situation in one of my overseas postings that I had been assigned to report on. Doing so necessitated setting aside the preconceptions I had brought to the situation and looking at what was actually there. Actually, in writing the book I had to set aside not only my own preconceptions but also those of the authors whose works I drew on. Concretely, it involved prying the data out of the frameworks in which these authors presented them, so that I could rearrange them into patterns that were satisfactory to me. It reminded me of prying ice cubes out of their form in a refrigerator tray.

Just as in the Foreign Service I needed to be concerned with the policy relevance of what I was reporting, that is, its relevance to the interests of the United States, so my concern now was with how the historical patterns I was discerning related to the church's transition from its original spiritual strength to its present—at least in the West—spiritual weakness. More particularly, it was to ascertain the extent to which this transition could be accounted for in terms of my transposition to post-biblical history of the theme that I had discerned in biblical redemption history. As will be recalled, this theme was that power lies ultimately in acceptance of our powerlessness, the only true power being not ours but God's. As transposed, it was that just as when the church lacks material power it is powerful spiritually, so when it acquires material power it loses spiritual power. In the previous chapter, I spoke of what I was doing in the book as in a sense extending biblical redemption history into the post-biblical period. As I proceeded along this line, it came to me how so momentous an undertaking could in fact be carried out. It was by asking of the events being dealt with what I have termed the "redemption history" question: Where is the Lord in this, as Judge and as Redeemer? This question applies to the events of personal as well as of collective history. In the church's transition from spiritual power coupled with material powerlessness to material power coupled with spiritual powerlessness, the hand of the Lord, who alone is powerful, may indeed be seen.

In sum: the book succeeded in connecting the present-day church with its material power but spiritual weakness to its starting point in the early church with its material weakness but spiritual power. Somewhat as Magellan's crew did in sailing around the world, it arrived back at its starting point. It did this by virtue of two things: One was the theme of "power lies ultimately in acceptance of our powerlessness" that I had discerned in biblical redemption history and now in its transpositions traced through subsequent history. The other was the skills and disciplines that I had acquired in the Foreign Service, thereby demonstrating the crucial point of their pertinence. Already, in that book's Prologue, I made explicit the value of secular disciplines in discerning and comprehending the biblical tradition and subsequent history. But even while demonstrating the possibility of this circumnavigation, the book did so imperfectly. First, in its focus on church-state relations as the key—a natural one for a Foreign Service Officer—it slid over theological developments also central to the story. Second, it treated the contribution of secular disciplines as only the passive one of enabling the investigation of historical developments. This was consistent with my then idea that the church could be restored through an awareness of its narrative—an identity narrative. It did not, however, take account of their vital active role of elucidating the signs of revelation to be found in these developments. Necessarily, it did not consider the basis of these disciplines, how they are acquired, what they can contribute, or within what limits they need to be kept either. These things, however, are the concern of the present book, for which that one, while laying an indispensable foundation, left more than sufficient scope.

Properly into Theology

The four years that I spent in Wycliffe were still not sufficient to finish the writing of that book. Nor was an additional year in England, this one not in Wycliffe but in Tyndale House in Cambridge, an institution devoted to biblical research but accommodating me as an exception. But I got far enough with it that I could carry on back in America, still under McGrath's supervision. Finally, some twenty-five years after the idea for it had come to me, the book was complete.

The problem, then, was to get the manuscript published. McGrath as my mentor readily gave me his endorsement, and I thought that with so eminent a backing, finding a publisher would not be difficult. Once the book appeared, now possessing an *imprimatur* lacking for my pre-England attempts, no doubt it would become a best seller. I sent the manuscript off successively to prominent publishers of such books, only again to receive successive rejection slips. I began to wonder whether my twenty-five-year investment in the book was largely in vain, whether the futility that overhung me in the wake of my mandatory retirement might be engulfing me after all. This proved to be not at all the case, but how it did had best be told in the next chapter.

9

Still Further into Theology

THE PREVIOUS CHAPTER REVOLVED largely around my connection with Alister McGrath, Britain's pre-eminent theologian, and how through him and through being in Oxford I was able to give depth to my book *To Restore the Church* and to carry it through to completion. In this chapter the central role will be that of Stanley Hauerwas, a similarly pre-eminent theologian in America. Thanks to him I could continue the process, so well begun under McGrath, of acquiring a theological competence. By virtue of it, when Hauerwas issued his challenge to me to "write something about the Foreign Service and theology," I had the means to respond. In so doing, I found that I was not only remedying deficiencies in my previous book but also opening the way to the Barthian natural theology I spoke of in the Prologue, through drawing on my Foreign Service disciplines. Opening the way to it, and also to things following from it, came into view as the *telos*, the underlying purpose, of this book and in large measure of my life too. The story of how all this came to pass is roundabout, necessarily so, and it is worth telling. I will begin with how I established contact with Hauerwas. I have told something of it already in the Prologue, but a fuller account is necessary to show how remarkable it was.

In the face of successive rejections by the publishers to whom I submitted my previous book, I began to despair. In my quandary, I sought the advice of a clergyman who I had long known, now become a retired bishop and himself a published author. His response was to ask which American theologian I had found to be most in accord with my own thinking as reflected in my book. From that theologian, he said, I should seek an endorsement. At first I could not think of any such. But then an outside possibility came to mind: Stanley Hauerwas. Why I thought of him at all is already sufficiently strange. In the previous chapter, I tell of my year in Tyndale House in Cambridge, 1992 to 1993. At the time the concept of narrative theology was being bandied about. Its premise was that narrative rather than propositional statement was the form best suited to convey essential truths; indeed, the Bible consists mostly of narrative. Having heard of it and wanting to know more, I inquired about it of a scholar at Tyndale House whom I happened to hear mention that he was working on the subject. He recommended two books: one was called *Why Narrative?* and the other was one whose title and author I have forgotten. *Why Narrative?* was not in when I checked for it in the Cambridge University library so I settled for the other—it did not impress me.

I thought no more about narrative theology at the time, and my inquiry into it might have ended there except for an occurrence in the library of my own seminary a couple of years later, after my return to America. I had gone there looking for a book of another sort, which I had not found. The library was about to close and I was reluctant to come away empty-handed. As I tried to think what else I might check out, *Why Narrative?* popped into my mind. I found it at the last possible minute. In contrast to the narrative theology book I had read in Cambridge, it was full of meaningful insights. One that struck me particularly was the idea that identity needs to be expressed in narrative form. And to be fully meaningful, an individual identity narrative needs to be set in an overarching narrative: a metanarrative. I spoke previously of how, once the narrative of the church's history began to take on form in my mind, I saw the possibility of my own life constituting a narrative, and of how this possibility gave me a sense of wholeness that I had not had before. I was struck by the extent to which my life experience accorded with the dynamic which *Why Narrative?* set out. Having had little idea of this or any other aspect of narrative theology until then, I thought myself to be like the protagonist in Molière's comedy *Le bourgeois gentil'homme,* who had spoken prose all his life without knowing it. This book, notably, is mainly in narrative form.

Why Narrative? was not by Hauerwas, but he had edited and contributed to it. As Professor of Theological Ethics at the Divinity School of Duke

University in Durham, North Carolina, he was already eminent (although not so eminent as he was later to be; he, too, became a Gifford Lecturer). Thus he should be in a position to help me find a publisher for my book, in accordance with the retired bishop's expectation. So I hied myself down to the Duke Divinity School, driving there from my home outside Washington, DC. I had no appointment, and in my urgency I did something the like of which I had never done before, and am unlikely to do again. Early in the morning, I stationed myself in the Divinity School parking lot, waited until he drove up and got out of his car (recognizing him from a book jacket photo), and approached him. Would he be too busy to see me, I wondered, or would he simply brush me off? As it turned out, he gave me a time later that day when I could come to his office. There I told him of my connection with McGrath, which seemed to interest him. He undertook to read the manuscript of my book, which I had brought with me. And he did read it, going on to supply me with a "blurb" for the book's back cover. That he took on board someone as unlikely as I—without academic credentials and thirteen years his senior—speaks of his goodness of heart. Some time later, when I told him the full story of how I made my connection with him, he said it was almost enough to make him believe in predestination; one thinks also of providence acting here.

I supposed that with his endorsement, as well as the one that McGrath had already given me, I would at last succeed in getting my book published. So I resumed submitting the manuscript to likely–seeming publishers. To my dismay, the response was no better than before. Evidently, the endorsements of world-famous theologians were not sufficient, at least for a book by an unknown author that did not fit easily into any of the conventional categories. An established reputation or a recognizable institutional position seemed also to be required. This was a further discouragement, coming on top of those I had received all along in my Foreign Service career and the rejection slips the book had already elicited.

However, it may also be seen as having served a positive purpose. For as detailed in the previous chapter, that book along with its important strengths had serious deficiencies, and had it been published at that time I might not have become aware of them, at least not in the way that I now have. And in supplying them as it is undertaking to do, this book will serve as the introduction to that one which at the time I was not capable of producing. More that this, it will open the way to the Barthian natural theology that we have been aiming for and to all that follows from it, for the world as well as the church. As for why I did not then have this capability, in the last chapter I told how Alister McGrath waited twenty years—until he could become thoroughly versed in theology—to embark on his enterprise of bringing the natural sciences into relation with it. I had no alternative except to learn theology in the course of bringing it together with my Foreign Service disciplines. Thus what I came up with in that book was bound to fall short. I trust, though, that twenty years after its completion, my theological competence is now sufficient.

This is not to say that my labors on that book were in vain; they put me in direct and ongoing contact with two of the world's leading theologians, first McGrath then Hauerwas, and with some less famous as well. This meant that I could present my ideas to them as well as receive theirs. The Foreign Service equivalent would be having the ear of the Secretary of State from time to time. Experiencing the brilliance of their minds at first hand has been enormously stimulating. Further, through writing that book I learned a vast amount and was positioned to learn a vast amount more.

I have a confession to make here—an awkward one. Once Hauerwas had given me his commendation and being still unaware of what beyond narrative theology he might have to offer, it crossed my mind that I no longer needed to bother with him. But I decided that would not be right, whether or not it would profit me. Had I not so decided, I would have made perhaps the worst mistake of my life. For as I have said, it was through him that the deficiencies in my theological knowledge began to be remedied, so that setting my present book in its proper theological context became a possibility. And through him, I was able to continue the process of acquiring general theological knowledge. What this process consisted of merits further explanation. It can be put in terms of the concept of crafts, or aspects of it, as advanced by Alasdair MacIntyre, the distinguished philosopher whose thought has deeply influenced many theologians, not least Hauerwas himself. MacIntyre's concept in fact underlies my subsuming of secular professions and occupations in general under the rubric of crafts.

As examples of crafts, MacIntyre has cited furniture making, fishing as it is or was carried on by New England fishermen, and even the doings of the Marine Corps. A craft, he has held, has its basis in a practice constituted by a particular tradition. It is a communal rather than an individual undertaking. Mastering it is not something one can do by oneself. Instead, it requires formation in the traditions and practices of the craft by those already versed in them, as in the apprenticeships served in medieval craft guilds.

Naturally, experience of practicing the craft for oneself is also required. In accordance with this concept, mastering theology is not something one can do on one's own. That I have in some measure mastered it is thanks to the immense privilege of being formed by McGrath and Hauerwas and to their willingness to devote time and effort to me.

MacIntyre's concept has a further significance, as those with a Foreign Service background may be surmising. The Foreign Service, the features of which I describe at some length in the Prologue, meets the above craft criteria, as no doubt do many other professions and occupations. It is not a collection of individuals but instead an organization and in some senses a community. It has a distinctive body of traditions and practices developed in the face of the exigencies of foreign relations that it has been called on to respond to. One cannot learn in advance how to be a competent Foreign Service officer, nor is it possible to become one overnight. Instead, many years are required to develop the necessary skills and disciplines, through practicing them under supervisors themselves formed in them, the equivalents of the medieval master craftsmen. At least this was the case with me, as is apparent from the previous chapters. The conclusion that the Foreign Service constitutes a craft has important implications. In fact its significance for natural theology is profound, as discussed in the Prologue. This book's elaboration of these implications gives it its main claim to significance.

Reverting to Hauerwas, in order to convey at all adequately what he has done for me, I must speak of the background out of which he came. He grew up in a small Texas town; he is indelibly Texan, as he himself insists. His father was a bricklayer, and under his father's tutelage in his teens he practiced the craft himself, acquiring no small proficiency in it. His loyalty to this, the craft of his initial formation, may play a part in traits that might otherwise be puzzling. The profanity that he has not infrequently used could as bricklayers' language signify his continuing attachment to it. His non-establishment origins have given him a standpoint from which the lapses from authenticity of intellectual élites may be especially apparent. With a bricklayer's forthrightness, he has not hesitated to call them out. The title of one of his books gives some of his flavor: *After Christendom: How is the Church to Behave if Freedom, Justice, and a Christian Nation are Bad Ideas?* Bricklaying was not his only formation, however. There was also his childhood attendance at his town's Methodist church together with the Christian faith manifested by his mother. These additional elements would

Still Further into Theology

have fostered his imagination, his capacity to dream, eventually to think in terms of the most refined images and ideas.

In writing in this book, I have been striving to be similarly loyal to the Foreign Service, the craft that formed me, and to be similarly faithful to what such loyalty entails. I have been at pains to refer the events and ideas I have spoken of to comparable elements of Foreign Service experience. To be sure, I will need to present theological concepts in terms receivable by academic theologians. But even with these, my concern is also to make them intelligible to those with backgrounds in the Foreign Service and other crafts. Hauerwas may have sensed that I, too, had a craft loyalty. This may have been among his reasons for taking on board someone otherwise so unpromising.

Although Hauerwas showed aptitude as a bricklayer, he did not long continue in that craft. In high school, his scholastic performance was noticed, and he was encouraged to go on to a university. After graduating from that he undertook the study of theology at the Yale Divinity School, as led perhaps by his Methodist upbringing and his mother's piety. Subsequently, he became himself an academic theologian, teaching for a number of years at Notre Dame University and then moving to the Duke Divinity School as its Professor of Theological Ethics. Despite the prominence that he has achieved, he has remained totally without pretension, along with his unflinching honesty. To cite one example, he was selected to be the 2001 Gifford Lecturer. As already alluded to, the Gifford Lectures, which have been given in Scotland for the last century and a half, have come to mark the summit of theological prestige. When I congratulated him on his selection, all he said was that it showed the selectors were scraping the bottom of the barrel.

Characterizing his thought is difficult if not impossible. His writing is both vast and various, and he has expressed himself for the most part in essays responding to particular questions, not in systematic expositions. His thought would probably not be susceptible to characterization anyway. Instead, apprehending it comes through exposure over time—as with Foreign Service disciplines. The one thing that can safely be said about it is that it is never safe. This is to say, it never follows conventional lines, lines that are part of the prevailing mindset and therefore less likely to be questioned. Instead, it cuts across these lines with uncommon insight, unerringly detecting their flaws. This probably is what has made him controversial for many, while at the same time giving him lasting influence over many more.

I will nevertheless venture what might be called a keyhole view of his thought: accurate so far as it goes but no more than indicative of what lies in the rest of the room. Among his basic themes is the centrality of the church in Christian understanding. He sees it as a community formed by the biblical narrative, centered on Jesus Christ and, in turn, forming its members in the virtues necessary to bear truthful witness to each other and to the world. Thus it is not to be accounted as beholden to any worldly systems or values but instead as having its own standing place. Consistent with this, it does not seek social or political power, so as to be able to "make history come out in a certain way." But neither is it indifferent to the social and political orders in which it finds itself. Instead, its role is to constitute a witness to state and society, modeling in its own life a different sort of community, one based not on coercion but on its formative narrative and the love of the other which this engenders. His concern for the suffering and for the mentally handicapped, about whom he has written at length, comes out of this approach, as does also the central importance he accords to pacifism. His pacifism does not preclude his pointed critiques of governmental and other secular institutions, including universities, which he sees as having bought into the liberal values of our time. By the term "liberal," he does not have reference to current political and social divisions but intends simply those ways of thinking which are premised on the autonomy and self-sufficiency of the individual and on the universality of human reason—on these shifting sand rather than on the constitutive narrative of the church.

Hauerwas' thought may be approached also through three main influences that he has acknowledged. In what I have already said about his thought, its accord with one of these three influences is particularly evident. This influence is that of the late John Howard Yoder, the brilliant Mennonite theologian who was his fellow professor at Notre Dame. The Mennonites come out of the Anabaptist tradition, of which I spoke in connection with my previous book's discussion of the Reformation (see this book's chapter 8). The Anabaptists reacted against the mainstream of the Reformation with its acceptance of a leading role for the state within the church. Thus they too understood the church as standing apart from established political and social structures—and were severely persecuted for it. Hauerwas' appropriation of this tradition is reflected particularly in his view of the church, one of the main strands of his theology.

All this may seem far afield from the world in which the Foreign Service moves. Indeed, it is somewhat at variance with my own standpoint as shaped by that craft. There is a remarkable intersection between the two, however. In chapter 8, I spoke of my discovery that the Anabaptist criticism of the role in the early church of the Emperor Constantine, and of state intervention in the church in general, accorded closely with mine. Constantine ended the centuries of Roman persecution of the church but also assumed a major role in its affairs. Thus both the Anabaptists and I, and Hauerwas too, may be considered anti-Constantinians. The Anabaptist view came out of the circumstances which gave rise to their movement, described above. My view comes out of my experience of establishment, governmental and institutional, acquired in and through the Foreign Service. Remarkably, the Anabaptists and I, proceeding from almost directly opposite starting points, have arrived at much the same place.

The influence of Alasdair MacIntyre is another that Hauerwas has spoken of as primary for him. We have already met MacIntyre in connection with his concept of crafts. More central to his thought is his contention that there is no truth that is not tradition-based. He sets this forth in such books as *After Virtue: A Study in Moral Theory* and *Whose Justice? Which Rationality?* Macintyre has made the case that there are traditions implicit even within the supposedly universal rationality which the Enlightenment propounded, namely those of the dominant social groupings in the West. Therefore, reason cannot qualify as universal, either socially or geographically. His contention, which at first may have seemed counter-factual, has won wide acceptance. This does not mean that truth is relative, however. On the contrary, it is to be taken as an encouragement to stand fast in a tradition-based truth, especially as it answers questions which other traditions are unable to resolve. Not surprising is Hauerwas' receptivity to MacIntyre's view, according as it does with his own account of the church as based on the biblical tradition. Again, his view may sound strange in ears such as are to be found in the Foreign Service. But surely those who have been formed in this craft can appreciate that it, too, has a tradition and that their rationality has needed to be exercised within it. They especially will have seen that ways of thinking that apply in the West, out of which they have come, more frequently than not are inapplicable in those parts of the world in which they have served.

Hauerwas' thought may be approached finally through another influence which he has acknowledged, in some way the most significant. It is that of Karl Barth, who is of special interest to us in view of the essential role he plays in this book. Although Swiss, Barth spent a large part of his career in Germany, where he stood forthrightly against the theological liberalism prevailing in the nineteenth and early twentieth century (and lingering on into the latter twentieth and early twenty-first). Barth's stand against Nazism as it took hold in the Germany of the 1930s, against which this liberalism provided scant defense, was no less forthright. Again, the term liberalism requires some clarification. In question was the liberalism that looked to philosophical systems and to human culture and reason as standards by which to judge revelation as set forth in Scripture. Barth contradicted this notion, asserting that revelation is self-authenticating and not dependent for validation on anything external to it. Probably most of us tend to look on it as dependent on these things. The concept of its independence can take us aback until we reflect that by making revelation and therefore God himself dependent on something else we are making that something else into God. The self-authentication of revelation complements MacIntyre's contention about truth being tradition-based, in that it provides a ground for accepting the truth that is based on revelation. This, in turn, supports Hauerwas' emphasis on the church as the community formed by the biblical narrative centering on Jesus Christ.

Notable as Hauerwas has been for his theological writing, in his teaching he has been no less so, although the nature of teaching makes it less likely to be known. Scores of his students have become witnesses to his deep and abiding influence on them. A special testimony to the effectiveness of his teaching is what it has done for me even at a distance. Apart from my meeting with him every year or so, his contact with me has been limited to e-mails. But by it he has pointed me to books I ought to read, sometimes his but mainly those of others, and has sent me essays and other writings of his as he produced them. In return, I have sent him my comments. To do this, I had not only to comprehend what he wrote but also to articulate my thoughts with clarity and coherence. I have had the privilege of a similar correspondence with McGrath. When responding to people of their intellectual caliber, one does one's utmost to be both coherent and succinct. I have been accordingly thankful for the schooling in written expression with which reporting from overseas in the Foreign Service provided me.

With Hauerwas, in the beginning I frequently betrayed my failure to grasp properly what he was saying, but this never discouraged him. And as time went on, I improved. Not long ago, when I sent him my comments on his *With the Grain of the Universe,* his Gifford Lectures in book form, he said they were the best he had received. Whatever kindly exaggeration may have been involved in his verdict, it testifies to an advance in my theological sophistication. It was through readings that he pointed me to that I became acquainted with many of the theologians whom McGrath was to discuss in his *Scientific Theology* series, cited in chapter 8. By virtue of this acquaintance I was able to understand rather well what this seminal work said.

Hauerwas passed on to me his principal influences, most of whom I had been little aware. I did not get my anti-Constantinianism from Yoder; I already had it. But he confirmed me in my espousal of it and supplied me with additional grounds for adhering to it. Further, he enabled me to see the coherence of the Mennonite view of state and society from the standpoint of the Anabaptist/Mennonite tradition, even while not quite persuading me to adopt it. I have indicated already how Alasdair MacIntyre's concept of crafts enabled me to identify the Foreign Service as a craft. It is thanks to this identification that my account of my career in it can make the major contribution to natural theology that I am claiming for it. But MacIntyre's contribution has not been limited to that. In his *After Virtue* and his *Whose Justice? Which Rationality?* he enabled me too to see the particularity of supposedly universal reason and the correlative necessity of tradition as the basis for truth. And along with him I now see this not as leading to some sort of relativism but rather as validating adherence to Christian truth.

But it is of Barth, above all, that I would speak of in this connection. To a large extent, his thought has become the basis of my own. It is substantially set forth in his *Church Dogmatics,* which at Hauerwas' instigation I read in its entirety. It consists of thirteen hefty volumes, plus an index. On the first try, I got through the first volume and a half, after a fashion. I tried again a couple of years later, and this time I got through all the way. The work consists of a more than thoroughgoing exposition of the church's basic doctrines: the Trinity, creation, election, redemption, reconciliation, and so forth, these in relation to biblical revelation and also to the thought of the early church, the Middle Ages, and the Reformation, especially the latter. It did not so much change my concepts as deepen them, showing them to have dimensions that I had not previously been aware of. And it enabled me to know finally where I stood, in the face of opposing theological positions.

Its significance for our present undertaking is what concerns us here. Our undertaking is to determine not only the applicability of Foreign Service disciplines to theology but also how they should be related to theology. As already noted, Barth's consistent premise is the self-authenticating nature of biblical revelation. This might seem to preclude the application to theology of Foreign Service disciplines as also those of other secular crafts. In fact, Barth himself thought so. Actually, his premise is necessary for their applicability in that it sets a limit for them which validates their application, as will be elaborated in the Epilogue. Most theologians have supposed that there is no possibility of their conforming to this limit, that in order for the world's contribution to be applied to theology it has to be set aside. But as argued in the Prologue, the craft concept as instantiated in the Foreign Service and elsewhere points to how this can be done, thereby making a contribution to natural theology of cardinal importance in its own terms as well as those of the church and the world.

What is truly extraordinary in my case, and perhaps indicative of Hauerwas' impact on his regular students, is his urging me to write the present account of the links between Foreign Service disciplines and theology. I spoke of this already in the Prologue. For fifty years, I had not only wanted to write such an account but had felt that I ought to, yet I found no satisfactory way of doing it. I had all but given up. But in the wake of his urging a way came to me, namely to tell the story of how I came upon these links in the course of my Foreign Service, as I have been doing, and then to draw their implications, as I will be doing in the Epilogue. For his grasp of what I wanted to do and also the importance of it there is no ready explanation. He has not had professional experience of an organization much like the Foreign Service, nor has he developed any systematic and extended account of natural theology of his own. The Anabaptist tradition, which he has incorporated into his thinking, would not seem to afford much place for it. His own appropriation of Barth would not have led him in this direction either. Barth vehemently rejected the idea of a natural theology. Therefore, only by a brilliant intuition could he have discerned the potential that he did, in the subject and in me. This may be seen as the work of the Holy Spirit, operating as he did at Pentecost, in the fashion to be described in the Epilogue.

The story I set out to tell, the story of the journey in the course of which I came upon these links between the Foreign Service and theology and of the excitement I found in them is now at an end. The story makes evident that the journey entailed personal costs though not entirely, since it only alludes to those that fell on my family. At the same time, it has brought me abundant rewards. I am not constrained to dissemble my Foreign Service accomplishments or lack thereof, as some in their retirement seem to be. Instead, I am free to describe my career as it actually was, as I have here been doing. Rather than only reminiscing about a past that is no longer available, I am in a place where I do not have to leave my Foreign Service disciplines behind. Instead, I can and must draw on them fully as I deal with the even

Still Further into Theology

more compelling issues with which I am now confronted. I speak here especially of those arising in the formulation of the Barthian natural theology spoken of above, permitting the world properly to be related to the church, at which this book has been aiming and with which its Epilogue will be concerned. Paraphrasing Star Trek, it will necessitate boldly going where we and even the world's great theologians have never gone before. And these issues, instead of being ephemeral—as those arising in the Foreign Service— are abiding. I think that perhaps the fascination that the Foreign Service has held for me as for others has flowed from an inherent connection, not consciously recognized but vital, between issues its members deal with and theology. If so, in turning to theology I have turned to the fountainhead of this fascination. In doing so, I have found not just the life after the Foreign Service which my friends in the Paris embassy asked me about as related in the Prologue. I have found a measure of blessedness.

But if the rewards my journey has yielded are to be enjoyed only by me, its costs will not have been justified. For this to take place, it will have to yield a harvest reapable by others as well. A Barthian natural theology, together with what follows from it, would constitute this harvest. Establishing its feasibility will be our task in the Epilogue, which follows.

Epilogue

THE STORY I HAVE been telling—the story of my discovery of the links between theology and the Foreign Service in the course of my Foreign Service career—may be of human interest, at least I hope so. However, if it is only that, it will justify neither the costs of this discovery nor the continuing attention of the reader. To fulfil these requirements, these links will have to have significance for the world no less than for theology; in fact, for both it will have to meet a critical need. This significance is to be found, I believe, in the Barthian natural theology which these links make possible and which can be established on no other basis. For such a natural theology not only will address a central theological issue hitherto unresolved, it will have major implications for the world and for the church, too. The elaboration of this natural theology and its implications will be the concern of this Epilogue. It will necessitate entering a terrain unfamiliar to all but academic theologians, causing most others and even some of them to hesitate. As a non-academic, I have run no small risk in undertaking to cultivate and fructify it. But here we may call upon the central ethos of the Foreign Service: a willingness to face any challenge no matter how daunting, to accept any assignment no matter how difficult. No less may we draw on the example of Abraham and the other heroes cited in chapter 11 of the Letter to the Hebrews, who "by faith" risked venturing from the familiar, as Abraham did from Haran (Genesis 12), into the unknown. We may look also to Apolo Kivebulaya, who as related in chapter 6 gazed from the Uganda side of Africa's Great Rift Valley at the Congo lying opposite terrified—but who crossed it and went on into the Congo anyway. Hebrews 11 was Apolo's favorite biblical

Epilogue

passage; "by faith" translates into *kwa imani* in Apolo's Swahili. For unless we, too, leave behind the familiar and venture forth, this central theological issue will remain unresolved, the consequences flowing from its resolution for the world and the church will not be realized. Finally, we will not have shown that the disciplines of the Foreign Service and other secular crafts have indeed a vital contribution to make to theology.

First, though, we will need to take cognizance of a fundamental contradiction in which we appear to have landed ourselves. This contradiction was apparent already in the Prologue. There I advanced certain theological premises as necessary for our undertaking. Essentially these were the premises of Karl Barth, the pre-eminent theologian of the twentieth century (and necessarily better known to academic theologians than to others), which in turn reflected those of the Reformation. As already related, it was in the context of his theology that my own inquiring came to rest. I asserted that only if they accorded with these premises could the links we would be adducing between theology and Foreign Service disciplines be valid, that if they accorded instead with some others they would remain only superficial. In order so to accord, these links would have to leave theology undistorted by the world, here represented by the Foreign Service, and yet provide for theology's close association with the Foreign Service *qua* world. And herein lies the problem. Central to our premises is the self-authenticating nature of revelation, revelation as set forth in Scripture. This is to say of it that it is self-sufficient, requiring no validation from reason or any other human resource. Indeed, if such validations are adduced they can only distort it, dissipating its power. Yet all along we have been discerning how craft disciplines such as those of the Foreign Service can illuminate revelation, clarifying and deepening its meaning. Thus we will have to show how this illumination is, after all, consistent with revelation's self-authentication—how it can enhance revelation without subverting it—if our enterprise is not to fall to the ground and, in so doing, to leave unmet the critical need of theology and the world that we are positing. On the other hand, in showing the consistency of this illumination, we will have opened a new vista for theology, particularly for natural theology (as before taking nature as broadly equivalent to the world), and for the world too. Enfolded in this vista will be the means for meeting the critical need of each, justifying both my discovery's cost and the reader's perseverance. On this account, the overcoming of this contradiction will be integral to our development of a Barthian natural theology.

Theology and the Disciplines of the Foreign Service

The Critical Need in Question

What, then, is the critical need of the world and theology that we are positing, the meeting of which will have major implications for both? Our contention is that this need is for meaning, the most essential attribute of all. But this implies that both the world and theology are presently lacking in it, which is far from self-evident. Indeed, many would dispute this assertion. Therefore, before elaborating our Barthian natural theology, we will need to consider the matter with some care. We will consider the world first.

The world's primary need may be seen as the overcoming of the meaninglessness that dogs its doings. This statement, a sweeping one, entails that the world lacks meaning in itself, the world in itself being a world without deity. The atheists, the deniers of deity, in fact vouch for this, holding that the world—indeed the universe—is the product of mere chance and not a very happy product either, given all the world's problems. The celebrated atheist Richard Dawkins' book title, *The Blind Watchmaker*, was meant to bring out this randomness. Randomness implies an absence of goodness. The intensity with which worldly power is sought indeed testifies to the world's meaninglessness, for power affords within the world an appearance of the meaning which all people need. That worldly power is an appearance only is not however the way it is ordinarily viewed, is not the conventional wisdom. Thus here too further consideration is called for.

Worldly power may be regarded as of two main types, economic and political, both consisting in control or at least influence over others. Economic power seems the more widely sought. It may be acquired through establishing an enterprise of one's own or through ascending the corporate ladder (though not, its salaries being what they are, the Foreign Service ladder). And great efforts are made to obtain it. To be sure, material wealth affords a substantial degree of control over others. But many have testified to its emptiness once obtained. Others seek to counter this emptiness by acquiring still more wealth. In the longer term, though, they necessarily fall short.

Worldly power can be sought also through political means, that is, through government. The Foreign Service is open to being so used in that it wields influence over the destinies of nations, as we have seen. Something similar may be said of other government agencies. Perhaps more directly associated with worldly power is elective office. The pursuit of this can be intense, particularly at the higher levels, as presidential campaigns vividly illustrate. Such power, while it is held, may seem profoundly meaningful; hence, the intensity with which is not only sought but also held onto. But

Epilogue

it is necessarily transient. If it is held as a member of the Foreign Service or some such government agency, retirement brings it to an end. Elective offices have their terms and so are subject to being contested. And this limits the power that the occupants can wield as well as providing for their eventual removal. So the meaning which political power affords is circumscribed as well as transient.

To be sure, such power may be sought for other than its own sake. It may be sought also for the promotion of goals or principles held to be in the general interest. The general interest can be only a façade for the pursuit of self-interest. But it is not always or entirely so. To the extent to which it is not, it affords a mitigation of meaninglessness. But in this case it involves the importation of values not to be found in the world in itself, and therefore a transcending of the world itself.

In fact, there is a third avenue to meaning within the world. Craftsmen like stone carvers or furniture makers can find their craft highly meaningful, requiring their full concentration on it. Musicians—vocal and instrumental—painters, sculptors, and writers may be intensely devoted to their arts. Scholarship and science can call forth similar commitment. At the Goddard Space Center in Beltsville, Maryland, I once heard a talk by a scientist who was investigating radiations emanating from the early stages of the universe. He spoke of how much he looked forward to his work each day. But here, no less than in the case of power used for worthwhile ends, such enthusiasm depends on the importation of values from beyond the world. The scientist in question, although he did not articulate it, may be supposed to have sensed the Author of the Big Bang as ultimate source of these radiations. And if extra-worldly (i.e., divine) values are implicit in the excitement felt by such people, it seems only fitting to make them explicit, which is what a Barthian natural theology is about.

Of course, meaning within the world can be sought by relinquishing individual power as well as by exercising it, in the subordination of oneself to some larger entity: an organization or, above all, the nation. In this case, the entity becomes an end in itself, with its own brand of theology. When such a theology is devoid of the divine, as it was in Nazi Germany or the communist Soviet Union, not only are its results devastating, its futility becomes unmistakable.

To be sure, the establishment of a valid connection between theology and the world such as we are envisaging would not immediately overcome the world's meaninglessness. Neither would it provide answers to all the world's problems. Instead, it would likely operate at first at the margins, conferring a measure of meaning on activities and tasks otherwise no more than routine. While it would not answer the world's problems directly, it would afford a space both outside the world and connected to the world, in which answers might be worked out.

In the case of theology's critical need, the paradox is even greater: how can that which must be regarded as the ultimate repository of meaning be itself in need of meaning? There is no intention here to deny the meaningfulness of theology. But theology stands in a dual relation to the world, as we have seen. It must not allow itself to be taken over by the world, so as to lose its distinctiveness and thus its power. At the same time, it does not exist just for its own sake, but also for the world's sake; if cut off from the world, so that it no longer brings its distinctive perspective to bear on the world and its activities, it cannot but wither. Hence theology contains a need for a valid connection with the world such as we aim to provide, if it is to retain its full meaning.

A Brief History of Natural Theology

Theology itself has not been without recognition of this need. Nature, taken as including not just physical phenomena but also the human activities that are our focus, has been a concern of theology all along. Indeed, from certain standpoints nature as in "natural theology" has been its central concern. Already in the ancient world, the Church Fathers were grappling with the question of how they should relate those elements of pagan thought and culture that they perceived to be good to their faith. This concern was implicit in the writings of the Apologists of the second and third centuries— not apologizing for Christianity but rather justifying it to non-Christians. Justin Martyr (martyred c. 163 AD) thought it appropriate to draw on Stoic and Platonic concepts in his treatises on the superiority of Christianity to pagan philosophy. Tertullian, for his part, opposed any such approach, asking, "What has Athens to do with Jerusalem, or the [Platonic] Academy to do with the Church?" Nevertheless, in his *Apology*, composed around 200 AD, he shows his close familiarity with Roman jurisprudence as he tellingly demonstrates the incongruity of its principles with the Roman persecution of the church. Implicitly in this work, he was not only appealing to pagans on the basis of elements in their own thought and culture, he was also encouraging Christians to stand fast against persecution, confirming

Epilogue

the rightness of their faith despite the disdain of the world around them. In the latter, he may be seen as anticipating the drawing on secular disciplines that we are proposing as the resolution of the problem of natural theology.

Augustine, whose paramount importance was noted in the Prologue, dealt with the question directly in his writings some two hundred years after Tertullian. Taking as his paradigm the biblical "despoiling of the Egyptians," in which the Israelites in their exodus from Egypt prevailed on the Egyptians to "lend" them their ornaments, Augustine had this to say.

> If those who are called philosophers, particularly the Platonists, have said anything which is true and consistent with our faith, we must not reject it, but claim it for our own use, in the knowledge that they possess it unlawfully. The Egyptians possessed idols and heavy burdens, which the children of Israel hated and from which they fled; however, they also possessed vessels of gold and silver and clothes which our forbearers, in leaving Egypt, took for themselves in secret, intending to use them in a better manner (Exod 3:21–22, 12:35–36) ... In the same way, pagan learning is not entirely made up of false teaching and superstitions. It contains also some excellent teachings, well suited to be used by truth, and excellent moral values ... Now these are, so to speak, their gold and their silver, which they did not invent themselves, but which they dug out of the mines of the providence of God, which are scattered throughout the world ... The Christian, therefore, can separate these truths from their improper associations, take them away, and put them to their proper use for the proclamation of the gospel. (*De Doctrina Christiana*, II.xl.60-1, cited in McGrath, *A Scientific Theology,* vol. 1: *Nature*, page 14; Grand Rapids: Eerdmans, 2001.)

We may regard this as an excellent statement of the link between theology and the world—as far as it goes. What it fails to explain is, first, how these pagan "truths" are to be discerned as true and thus serviceable for the proclamation of the gospel and, second, how once put to use in proclamation they can be supportive of it without taking over from it. These same two questions, that is, of the serviceability and the safety of natural theology, have remained unanswered down to our own time. In fact, they were at the center of Karl Barth's concerns about natural theology, as we will see. We ourselves will have to answer them before the link between the world and theology that we are presenting can be regarded as valid.

First, however, we need to continue our glance at natural theology's development. It has academic dimensions, and for readers without formal theological training, including probably most of my former Foreign Service colleagues, these may make its development somewhat difficult to follow. But at least an acquaintance with these dimensions is required for an understanding of the potential of the disciplines of the Foreign Service and other crafts to contribute to theology. Further, a consideration of them is necessary if our analysis to have traction with academic theologians, as it must if it is to count as successful. Non-academic readers should consider themselves to be like Foreign Service Officers newly arrived at post and needing to devote themselves to the comprehension the country's political and economic complexities. Otherwise, for them the potential of craft disciplines to illuminate theology will only have been asserted. They will not with their own eyes have seen its authentication.

An account of the development of Christian theology was given already in the Prologue. Picking up from it, Augustine can be seen as failing to answer the questions of the serviceability and safety if natural theology in his theological writings generally, not just in his statement cited above. At the least, he appears to have allowed Platonic concepts into his theology to an extent sufficient to displace the biblical bias in favor of the poor and oppressed. Aquinas, the pre-eminent theologian of the Middle Ages, in his extensive drawings on the philosophy of Aristotle seems also to have been deficient in his criteria for the admission into church doctrine of humanly-originated concepts. Among such concepts as set forth in his great *Summa Theologiae* was natural law, knowable by human reason, as distinct from divine law, revealed by God. And this opened, or at any rate left open, the way for a human role in the attainment of salvation.

The Reformation's contribution to natural theology was however decisive. As we saw in the Prologue, its basic principle was that salvation, the deliverance from sin and death proclaimed by the New Testament, comes by faith, grace, Scripture, and Christ alone (in Latin *sola fide, gratia, Scriptura, Christo*) rather than being earned by the performance of righteous works. This was in opposition to the reliance on such works that had come to the fore the Middle Ages. The Reformation principle, affirming as it did the sole-sufficiency of divine grace, thereby stood squarely against any takeover of theology by concepts of human origin.

But the Reformation was not without regard for the world. Luther, its instigator, asserted the sanctity of secular occupations, previously regarded as of lesser worth, in accordance with this accepting a major role of the state in the governance of the church. Calvin, the great systemizer of

Epilogue

Reformation doctrines, at the very beginning of his magisterial *Institutes of the Christian Religion* spoke of the natural world as a "theater" displaying the glory of God to the eye of faith. These were important insights. Still, neither Reformer worked out the world's linkages with theology sufficiently to make his affirmation of the secular clearly congruent with the Reformation's *sola fide, gratia, Scriptura, Christo.* Instead, in the Lutheran tradition with its two "regiments," or spheres of competency, of church and state, the state was left to function in its own sphere largely apart from the church's, as secular occupations in general were left in theirs. Calvin, who was similarly affirming of the secular, in the links he made with theology was concerned more with the physical side of nature than with that of human activities, on which we are focusing. In the absence of a clear congruence with the world, the *sola fide* principle came under questioning from the world, the world seeing itself as having been left on its own to account for itself. And in so accounting, the world went off in directions of its own, the state casting itself as a final end and secular occupations becoming devoted to their autonomously determined objectives. These may be regarded as among the factors which occasioned the secularly oriented eighteenth-century Enlightenment. And the Enlightenment, which took human reason as its ultimate standard, culminated the derogation of *sola fide*. In this Epilogue, we will be undertaking in effect to complete what the Reformers left unfinished, so as to allow the full congruence of secular occupations with their *sola fide*.

An effect of the above development, as the Enlightenment unfolded, was a shift in the focus of natural theology to physical nature seen as having revelatory power in itself, albeit complementing biblical revelation. Probably the most notable exponent of this approach was William Paley, who in his book, *Natural Theology*, argued from the indications of design in nature to the existence of a Creator. In the nineteenth century he was overtaken by Darwin with his theory of evolution and by questions that the argument from design failed to answer as well. Also in the nineteenth century, natural theology further shifted its focus, or rather increased its focus on a shift already under way. This was in the direction of the philosophies and ideologies then in vogue, such as those of Kant and Hegel and of the newly ascendant nation-state, which as human constructions necessarily privileged the human over the divine. And this new focus, partaking of a shift in kind, was gathered up into theology itself, which increasingly looked to the human intellect and human nature for its concepts of the divine-human relationship and of God himself. The nineteenth-century German theologian

Friedrich Schleiermacher provides an example of this approach, which we are regarding as the essence of theological liberalism. He selected the human sense of absolute dependence as the starting point of his theology. The approach exemplified by Schleiermacher was carried over into natural theology. It was against natural theology of this sort that Karl Barth in the early twentieth century reacted with the forcefulness described in the Prologue.

Perhaps in part because of Barth's objections, natural theology then fell somewhat into abeyance. But in the present century it has been renewed in a major way by the work of Alister McGrath featuring his concepts of *ancilla theologiae*, or handmaid of theology, and of natural theology as having a place within the framework of revelation (see chapter 8). These are the concepts, together with MacIntyre's of crafts as discussed in chapter 9, which we will employ in building on our chosen biblical foundation, the Pentecost event, a foundation which may be termed pneumatic—in the sense not of pneumatic tires but of the Greek word *pneuma*, meaning spirit, here the Holy Spirit. Without these concepts there would be no possibility of resolving the issues of the serviceability and safety for theology of secularly originated ideas, the issues which we saw Augustine as stopping short of addressing. But with them we can both usefully and safely draw on the disciplines to be discerned in the Foreign Service and other secular crafts in our resolution of these issues.

Barth's View of Natural Theology

Before formulating this resolution, however, we will need to revert to the earlier twentieth century, to the views of Barth concerning natural theology. For these views constitute the objections that we will have to overcome if our formulation is to claim validity. We will need also to examine the still famous 1934 exchange between Barth and his fellow Swiss theologian Emil Brunner relating to natural theology. Doing so will be somewhat tricky, though. For Brunner, in his relatively brief essay, "Nature and Grace," did not set out his views as fully as he was to do later on. Barth, to some extent, may have misunderstood him. Nevertheless, the exchange effectively conveys the views that Barth was concerned to oppose. At the same time, it brings out elements of Brunner's position which complement rather than contradict Barth's and to which we can appeal for support. Moreover, the issues it raised have still not been settled; discussion of them continues.

Epilogue

Unless our formulation affords a resolution of them, doing justice to both sides in the debate, it will lose much of its point.

In assessing Barth, we need to remember that he did not operate in a historical vacuum. On the contrary, he was confronted by the idolization of the nation which wrought such havoc in the first half of the twentieth century with its two World Wars and Holocaust, particularly in its German manifestation—a havoc bearing on foreign policy as well as theology. As already discussed, the philosophies and ideologies in vogue in Barth's time were liberal in the sense that they privileged the human over the divine. In fact, this privileging extended to the collective as well as the individual sphere, to society and the nation, although this seems less taken account of. In Barth's view, such liberalism had taken over theology to the near exclusion of revelation. This situation, besides leading to defective theology, had left the church with few resources to oppose not just the exaltation of the individual but also national idolization. The resulting theological void underlay in his view the readiness of the so-called German Christians, the larger part of church membership in the Germany of the 1930s, to take Nazi principles on board. As a theologian, he felt his task was to restore theology to its proper basis in the Reformation's *sola fide,* thereby freeing it from liberalism's thrall and enabling it to stand forth in its essential majesty and power.

This does not, however, mean that Barth never engaged directly with the political and social issues of his time. On the contrary, he was a leader of the segment of the German church, known as the Confessing Church, which unlike the German Christians openly opposed Nazism. In 1934, as the Nazis moved in on the church, the Confessing Church declared its opposition in its Barmen Declaration, of which Barth was the principal author. Still, the making explicit of the political and social critique so powerfully implicit in his theology has been left largely to others.

Even less does it mean that Barth's concerns were unwarranted. The take-over of theology by worldly concepts and cultural values leads to its vitiation and even perversion, as we have seen. Theology still needs to be related to the world, though. The question is how this should be done. And Barth, for all the indispensability of the magnificent theological structure that he erected, failed to address this question properly.

I will not pretend to give a complete account of Barth's position on natural theology; his thoroughgoing consideration of its issues precludes ready summarization. I hope still to convey its core. In terms of the questions which Augustine left unanswered and which we have regarded as basic, Barth denied both the serviceability of philosophical and other secularly derived ideas and their safety. His most extensive discussion of natural theology appears in his *Church Dogmatics*, especially volume 2, part 1. In it, the opposition he posits between natural theology and revelation is stark. This starkness led Brunner to reproach him for a kind of dualism. But the Reformation with its reliance *sola fide* rather than on any human power may be seen in this way too. Specifically, Barth's premise was that the only true knowledge of God is the knowledge which God himself wills to disclose. This being so, natural theology as outside revelation and thus distorted by the Fall is inevitably inadequate. Worse than that, it represents humanity's attempt to bring knowledge of God and revelation itself under its own control. This attempt arises from the perennial human desire, instanced already in the Fall, to be in control. In the Fall as narrated in Genesis 3 the desire was to be in control of the knowledge of good and evil resulting from the eating of the forbidden fruit. Grace, as given by God in his total freedom, necessarily runs counter to human control. Thus there is an essential enmity between humanity and grace. Natural theology, based on knowledge of God derived outside revelation and thus under human control, is humanity's attempt to assimilate and domesticate grace, and revelation too. Barth held that natural theology has operated this way from the beginning of the church, infiltrating its doctrines and substituting human concepts for them, and accordingly is the key to the church's vitiation. Therefore, it is to be opposed at all costs—scarcely an encouragement to us in our development of a Barthian natural theology.

Barth drew specific implications from his conclusions. One was that the use of natural theology in apologetics, that is, in presenting Christianity to non-Christians, was harmful and to be avoided. For to do so entailed presenting the faith to them in terms of knowledge that as unbelievers they already possessed. Even though analogies could be seen between their knowledge and that provided by revelation, this meant addressing them on the grounds of their unbelief and so taking unbelief seriously. Since these analogies inevitably fell short of revelation, it also meant failing to take faith seriously, in effect fobbing them off with an imitation of the real thing. And to take their unbelief seriously while not taking one's own faith seriously could only confirm them in their unbelief.

Again in line with his conclusions, Barth addressed those biblical passages usually considered to support a natural theology-based apologetics. Among those he pointed to were Psalm 19, which begins, "The heavens

Epilogue

declare the glory of God," and Acts 14, in which St. Paul in Athens cites Greek poets in support of his proclamation to the Athenians. In fact, Barth acknowledged a whole stream in the biblical literature which could be taken to support such an apologetics. He contended that this stream could be regarded as doing so only if its sourcing in revelation was overlooked. The Psalmist saw the heavens as declaring God's glory only because the God of Israel had first been revealed to him. Paul would not have been aware of the aptness of his citations from the Greek poets apart from his own faith in Christ, to which he was bearing witness for his Athenian hearers. Therefore, these passages did not support an apologetic use of natural theology, starting as it did from outside revelation.

As we have seen, the extremity of Barth's position is understandable given the type of natural theology with which he was confronted, namely that drawing on intellectual constructions amenable to human shaping. Further, his position was useful and even necessary in view of the havoc that this type had led to, not just in theology but in the world. It was not the only conceivable type, though. The one we will be developing draws instead on crafts (i.e., secular professions and occupations and their disciplines). That Barth did not take account of these may be due to his having only an ecclesiastical and academic career. He had wide interests, to be sure. Along with his devotion to Mozart he was credited with a detailed knowledge of even the American Civil War. Still he would have been largely unaware of crafts and their attributes. That an awareness of them would have led him to different conclusions is at least a possibility.

The Brunner-Barth Exchange

We still need to consider Brunner's controversy with Barth. From the standpoint of Barth's own position as outlined above, the exception that he took to Brunner's is not surprising. Although Brunner's theology had up to then been thought substantially in accord with Barth's, his essay entitled "Natural Theology" brought to light a serious divergence. In it, Brunner began by denying that there were two sources or norms for the doctrine that the church proclaimed, one in nature, human experience, or history and another in revelation. And he affirmed that man's original righteousness was completely lost in the Fall. On both points he was in accord with the Reformation's *sola fide* principle, which is to say that salvation comes solely through God's grace and is not at all a human possibility. Both points accord also with Barth's position. With regard to the created order though, Brunner's essay made two especially notable affirmations. One was that while evidences of the Creator are necessarily imprinted on his creation, they can be seen truly only when illuminated by Christ. The other was that the material elements in the created order, in contrast to philosophy and other intellectual constructions, are affected no more than slightly by the Fall. And in these affirmations he may have gone beyond Barth. They will, however, be important to us in the formulation of our own position.

In ascribing responsibility to even "natural man," meaning humans after the Fall, for his actions, Brunner definitely diverged from Barth. He held that it was ascribable because in the Fall the image of God in natural man (the *imago Dei* attested in Genesis 1:26), though badly marred was not totally destroyed. Consequently, humanity retained some ability to recognize the imprint of God remaining in his creation. Humanity's refusal to recognize it and to render to God the obedience to which it called it was thus wilful rather than the result of incapacity, and hence it was consciously sinful. In so saying, Brunner can be seen as pointing to not one but two sources of knowledge of God, one in revelation and one outside it (albeit he specified that only the first was salvific).

Additionally, Brunner attributed to natural man a capacity for words, the necessary medium of revelation. His formulation was, "The Word of God does not have to create man's capacity for words; he already has that capacity." Together with the above-identified consciousness of sin this capacity constituted a point of contact, a key term for Brunner, allowing God to impart his revelation to humanity. Brunner went on to assert the presence in the world of orders of creation. These consisted primarily of the family and of the state. He saw them as instituted by God as an aspect of his grace, so that even in its fallen condition, without acceptance of its redemption by Christ, humanity could be preserved. In the course of elaborating his views, Brunner allowed himself some comments on Barth's theology. While acknowledging that it had formidable strengths he attributed to it some serious deficiencies. His comments were not without patronizing overtones.

Barth's response, written as usual in German, was titled simply *Nein!* The vehemence of his objections to Brunner's position need not be attributed to the *ad hominem* in Brunner's comments, at least not primarily. More significant would be the fact that Barth had not yet had a chance to elaborate his own position on natural theology. In the face of the inroads in the church that the German Christians with their liberal concepts were making, he would have felt a need to stake out his position, pending the time when he could propound it in detail.

Barth did not dispute that Brunner had affirmed major Reformation doctrines. His point was their incompatibility with the positions that Brunner went on to take. For how, he asked, could the properties which Brunner attributed to humanity in its fallenness, notably a remnant of the *imago Dei* and a consciousness of its sinfulness, then be solely a matter of God's grace, as the Reformation affirmed? On the basis of a human possession of them, salvation would be in part a human work rather than *sola fide*. Brunner's orders of creation also concerned him. In conferring a divine commission on the state, as in effect they did, they opened the way to an idolization of the nation and its traditions. And the German Christians, consistent with their receptivity to the Nazi concept of a special role for the German *Volk*, had been quick to welcome this. Further, in his essay, Brunner had not presented any ultimate purpose for his orders of creation, such as awaiting humanity's full reception of Christ's redemption, nor had he cited any basis for them in Scripture. As for Brunner's point of contact anterior to revelation, Barth held that it was totally destroyed in the Fall. The Word of God had to re-establish it. If it had continued to be a human capability, God would not be sovereign and freely electing, as insisted on in the Reformation.

In the light of the Brunner-Barth exchange, the prospects for a valid natural theology may appear more unpromising than ever. We have already seen how categorically Barth rejected the possibility of it. And now, Brunner's attempt to provide the elements of one has been called into serious question by Barth. We will persist in our undertaking anyway, trusting that Barth's rejection may not have been as categorical as he made it out to be and that Brunner may after all have had a significant contribution to make.

Our Biblical Basis in Pentecost

Consistency with our theological principles requires that we provide a biblical foundation for our formulation of natural theology. For this we will not look, at least not primarily, to Psalm 19 and other psalms citing creation as attesting to God's glory or to St. Paul's quotation of the Greeks' own poets in support of his proclamation to the Athenians (Acts 17) although, as Barth noted, many have done so. Instead, we will turn to the Pentecost event, in which the Holy Spirit (hence the term *pneumatic*) took the leading role. This event played a special part in my own theological development, as related in chapter 3. More particularly, it provides the linchpin we need to hold the theological links with craft disciplines disclosed by my Foreign Service career together with the implications that we will be drawing from them.

The Pentecost event is described in chapter 2 of the Book of Acts. In brief, Acts tells how Jesus' disciples, gathered together in Jerusalem fifty days after his resurrection, are inspired to go forth and proclaim the wonderful works of God, that is, the gospel. As they do so, the bystanders, who represent a long list of nationalities, understand them as speaking in their own languages. The list does not seem to be random. Instead, it is explainable as pointing to the nations and places around the Mediterranean to which the gospel had spread by the time, perhaps around the year 80, that Acts was written down.

The Acts account emphasizes not only the intelligibility but also the intimacy for the bystanders of the disciples' proclamation, how they hear it as in their own languages "in which we were born." The emphasis on intimacy is surely significant. If we accept that the Acts account is anticipatory of the church's spread in the way that I have said, we will be impelled to regard it as meaning that the various peoples receiving the gospel in the ancient world heard it in terms not only of their own languages but also of their own traditions and experiences, of those things nearest them, at the surface of their consciousnesses or just under. Implicit in their hearing of it was the illumination by the gospel of these traditional and experiential elements, their arrangement into meaningful patterns in place of their previous randomness. One thinks of iron filings lying scattered on a sheet of paper and how they stand up and group themselves around the poles of a magnet held beneath them.

The Acts account itself describes such a transformation as having taken place in the consciousnesses of the Jerusalem bystanders. It tells how St. Peter, in confronting them with Jesus' death and resurrection, brought them to an awareness both of their need for redemption and of its possibility, through Jesus. They would not have perceived his death and resurrection as thus bringing into a pattern the various elements of their lives had they not been opened to this perception. And their opening to it, as also the opening of subsequent converts to their own lives' patterning, could not have been the work of their own hands or of any concepts which they already possessed. For these things provided no basis for it. Instead, it must have been wrought by the Holy Spirit, acting through Peter's proclamation.

Epilogue

If, through the Holy Spirit so acting, these elements were brought into a new light, we should not suppose that they were themselves left untransformed, any more than that Jesus left as water what he turned into wine at the Cana wedding (John 2). They would have become luminous in a way that they were not before and, still through the Holy Spirit, would have cast light on the gospel in turn. This illumination, clarifying and deepening the meaning of the gospel for those coming to belief, would have contributed importantly to its being spread by them so rapidly throughout the Roman Empire.

Nor is this Acts account the only place in the New Testament where such happenings occur. In chapter 12 of his first letter to his Corinthian converts, St. Paul speaks of various gifts which the Spirit has bestowed on them, so that they may build up the church: wisdom, knowledge, faith, healing, and others. These may be seen as coming out of the elements of their backgrounds and experiences that the Spirit had illuminated in the process of converting them.

This same phenomenon—of being illuminated and of illuminating in turn—is very much what we have seen as able to happen with the disciplines of the Foreign Service and other crafts. Most particularly, it is the phenomenon that I encountered in the course of my Foreign Service career. To take the initial, and in some ways primary, example, I was struck powerfully when I first came upon them by the affinities between the methods of modern biblical criticism and the critical approach into which I had been disciplined by the Foreign Service. As related in chapter 3, in this encounter it was as if scales fell from my eyes, and I saw the Scriptures for the first time not in black and white but in their original vivid colors. I would not have perceived these affinities or their significance had I not already been opened to them, had I not already believed. My opening to them was not my own doing—certainly I am neither wise nor worthy enough for that—nor was I prepared for it by any external influences or instruction. Therefore, I can account it only to the work of the Holy Spirit, touching my Foreign Service disciplines as in bringing me to belief he had touched me.

Incidentally, a division between subject and object, said to have arisen in Western culture, has been of concern to some theologians, including Emil Brunner. This division consists in the objectification of the faith so that it can be viewed with detachment by the subject, that is, the person perceiving it, and be comprehended by the intellect rather than the heart. But in our concept as set forth above, the division is overcome through the subsistence of both, the object and the subject, in the Holy Spirit. Accordingly, the perception and the person perceiving it are essentially one.

Barth, as we saw, considered natural theology as an attempt to bring revelation under human control. But, I would insist, my discovery of the affinities between biblical criticism and my own critical approach did not impel me to bring Scripture into conformity with my own ideas. On the contrary, in opening my eyes to the Scriptures as never before it subjected me to their control. Nor did the impact of my discovery stop there. It gave me my vocation, of which I had had only vague notions previously. This was to bring these same affinities to the consciousness of others, so that their eyes too might be opened to the Scriptures and to the gospel that they set forth. This vocation of mine was to be carried out by way of inviting others not compelling them; the exercise of any compulsion would have been unthinkable. This book in a sense culminates my vocation, on my fulfilment of which I am no doubt to be judged, and to be found as falling short. So we may with confidence say that natural theology need not be an attempt to bring revelation under human control, which was the core of Barth's concern about it. In fact, to suppose that it is essentially such an attempt is to misconceive its essential nature.

Herein may be seen the valid link between theology and disciplines as of the Foreign Service, the link allowing the illumination of theology by these disciplines as well as the illumination of these disciplines by theology, that we have all along been seeking. Moreover, this link provides for the Barthian natural theology which has hitherto been elusive and which has the major implications already cited. The dimensions of this natural theology will emerge as we consider how it surmounts Barth's specific objections while also according with important elements of Brunner's approach.

Overcoming Barth's Objections

This section especially tends towards the academic. But it is necessary. Without it the validity of our formulation of natural theology will not have been established, and the potential of craft disciplines to contribute to theology will not have been upheld.

As for Barth's objections, we have taken as the two basic issues of natural theology, both of which Augustine left unaddressed, its serviceability and its safety. That is to say, whether it can contribute to a true knowledge of God and whether, when called on to contribute, it will proceed to substitute itself for knowledge derived from revelation. As we have seen, Barth objected to natural theology on both scores. He considered that knowledge of God from a source other than revelation was deficient and therefore ought not to be resorted to. Further, once another knowledge was set alongside revelation, inevitably it took over from revelation. And in both his time and in our own his apprehensions have proved abundantly justified. In his, philosophies and other intellectual constructions privileging a human standpoint were setting the pace for theology; and in ours, the values of a similarly oriented culture have pervaded the church's proclamation, so that it is conformed to them rather than they to it.

What safeguards would our envisaged Barthian natural theology offer against the same thing happening when Foreign Service and other craft disciplines are drawn on to illuminate theological concepts? For that matter, how is it that in my discovery of the links between these disciplines and theology I had no sense of thrusting a Foreign Service model onto the church? Firstly, there is the necessary role of the Holy Spirit in the process, highlighted by our designation of the Pentecost event as our biblical foundation. In accordance with it, theology's links with these disciplines and the illumination they provide are discernible only to those who by the action of the Holy Spirit have come to believe. The disciplines, or elements of them, with which these links have been made will themselves have been touched by the Holy Spirit. And it is through their having been so touched that their ability to link with theology becomes discernible. Thereby these disciplines will be cast into revelation's mold, not revelation into theirs—the outcome that Barth so deplored. If this outcome, the casting of secular disciplines into revelation's mold, is granted, Barth's objections to the serviceability of natural theology fall away, too. For what has been touched and conformed by the Holy Spirit must also be able to illuminate revelation suitably.

In fact, Brunner came close to our point about the need of secular disciplines first to be touched by the Holy Spirit in his 1934 essay. Speaking of a revelation in creation, that is, in the natural order of things as created by God, he characterized it as "that which only he can recognize in all its magnitude, whose eyes have been opened by Christ." In parallel, we have said that the luminousness of secular elements can be recognized only through the operation of the Holy Spirit. This might be taken as saying the same thing, in view of the unity of Christ and the Holy Spirit with God in the Trinity. The respective emphases of the two formulations, Brunner's and ours, are however different. Having our eyes opened by Christ suggests that they are now to be used in the furtherance of rational inquiry, whereas the operation of the Holy Spirit speaks of ideas coming in from beyond ourselves—a more "pneumatic" concept.

There is a further safeguard against the taking over of revelation by concepts of secular origin. It lies in the special nature of crafts, the disciplines of which have been our focus. As discussed in chapter 9, stone carving, furniture making, glass blowing, and the like may readily be recognized as instances of crafts. We have also accounted the Foreign Service and other professions and occupations as among them, too. We analyzed them as characterized by the intractability—the inherent inviolability—of the materials they deal with. The properties of the stone that is carved, the wood that is fashioned, the glass that is blown cannot be altered by their fashioners to suit their own fancies. Instead, they must be taken as they are, in effect as they have come from the hands of the Creator, and their limits conformed to as they are worked on. Herein is the basis of the disciplines that crafts impose, by virtue of which we can speak of craft disciplines. The Foreign Service counterpart to this intractability of subject materials is the intractability of foreign relations. Some things can be accomplished in dealing with other nations but the limits are narrow. To be sure, the materials with which the Foreign Service deals, such as the ambitions and apprehensions of nations, are far from being as they have come from the Creator. Even so, they operate within frameworks that are by and large immutable. The ambitions and sensitivities of nations are largely constant. In international relations, as elsewhere, relying ultimately on one's own power is ultimately futile.

Again, Brunner may be adduced in support of our position, for with regard to the intractability of existing materials he said, "Apart from man the disturbance or derangement of the *natura*, the order of existence created by God, is, as it were, but a slight one." As for why this should be so, it may be seen as part of the covenant which God established with Israel and, through Israel, with the whole world. God's covenant made with Noah after the flood and presumably subsumed in his covenant with Israel, wherein he promised never again as in the flood to violate the natural order of things, is a further pointer in this direction.

By the intractability of their materials and the discipline which this entails, crafts are distinguished from philosophical systems and other intellectual constructions, the materials of which are amenable to human manipulation and thus do not impose disciplines of this sort. A partial

Epilogue

exception might be those philosophies rooted in a tradition arising out of the history of a people. Aristotle's philosophy, for example, had its basis the history of the ancient Greek city-state or *polis*. The eighteenth century Enlightenment, regarding tradition as a drag on freedom, rejected it in favor of sole reliance on a human reason, supposedly universal but actually itself bound to a particular tradition. Thus it allowed the human element, subject to the Fall, to play a key role in philosophical and ideological developments deriving from it. That the human element did play this role is evident from the inability of post-Enlightenment philosophies, effectively lacking a common standard to appeal to, to agree with each other on such basic concepts as justice. And, as we have seen, the influence on theology of these philosophies, privileging as they did the human over the divine, was Barth's particular concern.

A special feature of crafts affords still another safeguard. In chapter 9, we saw an equivalent of the Marxian concept of the surplus value created by labor. This was in the skills and disciplines that crafts generate when practiced with commitment. That is to say, these skills come to exceed what is required in the crafts generating them and for their fuller application must be applied elsewhere—the fullest application of all being to theology. In the Foreign Service, my reporting from overseas back to Washington developed my analytical and critical faculties. But only when I turned to biblical interpretation and to the comprehension of church history and doctrine did their full significance emerge. Actually, what I was applying in the latter fields was not my craft disciplines but rather distillations of them. In their distilled form, they became translatable, their applicability no longer confined to their original settings. As distillations rather than the disciplines, they further minimized the risk that they would transform theology into a secular craft—the outcome that Barth feared.

Admittedly, these safeguards are not absolute; nothing in this world is absolute. So they do not eliminate all risks. There are, however, marks—subjective and objective—indicating the genuineness of links perceived between craft disciplines and theology. Subjectively, concerning one's own perception of them, there is the excitement of discovery, entailing a desire to share it with others. In his *Letter to Simpliciamus* Augustine speaks of our delight in God's commandments as enabling us to perform them. Likely this delight is of much the same sort as our excitement of discovery. Objectively, in the case of perceptions of these links by people other than ourselves, the mark is that these people will only invite to a sharing in their discoveries;

they will never compel it. Of course, if this safeguard is to be effective, the theology with which links are made must be fully grounded in revelation as attested in Scripture. If it is not so grounded, the Holy Spirit will not have enabled the links, through whom this revelation came. The necessity of this grounding affords a further way to "test the spirits," as urged in the First Letter of John 4:1. And having been so tested, these links can then be regarded as indeed touched by the Spirit.

It may be added that natural theology, as we have developed the concept, has validation within Scripture itself. We have remarked on the Psalms featuring creation as reflecting the glories of the Creator and on St. Paul's appropriation of classic Greek poets in addressing the Athenians. As we saw, it was by virtue of the faith already imparted to them by the Holy Spirit that the Psalmists and Paul respectively perceived creation and the Greek poets as illuminating their proclamation.

There is a further evidence, perhaps less obvious. In both the Old Testament and the New, David is regarded as the paragon of biblical history. In the Old Testament, he is the king who, in contrast to his successors, walked consistently in the way of the Lord. In the New Testament, David is the progenitor and prototype of the Messiah. Yet in the surprisingly candid account of his reign in 2 Samuel and 1 Kings he does not seem so holy. The paradox is resolved, however, if we consider that the believers of both Testaments, themselves touched by the Holy Spirit, perceived his story as it was also so touched. Our concept may be seen as resolving a further biblical paradox. The New Testament is uncompromisingly non-violent, never supporting the use of force. Yet it draws on such military imagery as the helmet of salvation and the sword of the Spirit of Ephesians 6. But if it is seen as drawing not on the disciplines themselves of military crafts but rather on distillations of them, the paradox disappears.

Would Barth have been persuaded by our arguments? Would he have allowed that a natural theology was possible within his theological framework? Would he have admitted that craft disciplines such as of the Foreign Service can serve as the *ancillae theologiae*, the handmaids of theology, that we have considered them to be? Perhaps he would not have, in view of his unfamiliarity with crafts in the sense that we have been discussing. Nevertheless, he may not have been as resistant to natural theology as he seemed. This is indicated by his discussion of *vestigia trinitatis* or traces of the Trinity, the threefold Godhead of Father, Son, and Holy Spirit, which precedes that of natural theology in volume 1 of his *Church Dogmatics*.

Epilogue

In his consideration of the Trinity, Barth notes the prevalence of the number three in nature: the solid, liquid, and gaseous states of matter; the primary colors of red, blue, and yellow, among many other instances. In particular, he addresses an example adduced by the medieval theologian Anselm of Canterbury in connection with his own account of the doctrine. It is of spring, stream, and lake as being distinctive in themselves yet constituting a single river. He acknowledges that such major figures as Augustine and Aquinas have made use of these instances in their own discussions, albeit perhaps in their search for language adequate to express the Trinity. But he will not concede that the doctrine is derived from these instances, insisting instead on its Scriptural root. His fear here, as with natural theology, is that if these instances are used to explain the doctrine of the Trinity, they will come to be seen as its root and thus take over from revelation. So he counsels strongly against their use for this purpose. Nevertheless, he concedes that they might be appropriate for "interpretation" though not for "illustration," illustration in some measure constituting a defining of the doctrine. In Barth's concluding concession, we may see an opening for our formulation of natural theology. Our concept of worldly disciplines as clarifying and deepening theological concepts corresponds to the "interpretation" which he allows while avoiding the "illustration" which he eschews.

Moreover, as we saw above, Barth argued against a scriptural support for natural theology, as in Psalm 19 and Acts 14, on the grounds that the psalmist would not have seen the heavens as declaring the glory of God and Paul would not have recognized support for his proclamation in the Greek poets had they not already believed. Hence, they were not beginning from outside revelation but instead from within it. But this comes quite close to our own concept of the illumination of revelation by elements touched by the Holy Spirit, as perceived by those who are themselves so touched.

Finally, it is important to note the striking affinity of our concept of natural theology with Barth's of revelation. In discussing it, he adheres strictly to the "Scripture principle," the supremacy of Scripture over church and tradition. At the same time, he regards revelation as not simply a matter of the words in the Bible but instead as three-tiered. First, there is revelation itself, the word of God spoken to the prophets and apostles. Then, there is the witness to revelation by the prophets and apostles, in their human words reflecting aspects of their humanity—Barth holds that they do not cease to be human in their witness. Finally, there is the appropriation of their witness by its readers and hearers, whereby it becomes for them revelation. He sees each of the two movements involved—that from revelation to witness and that from witness to appropriation—as coming about through the operation of the Holy Spirit. Only through the Spirit's action can they validly take place. Likewise, it is through the operation of the Holy Spirit that in our concept of natural theology illumination successively takes place. From those touched and converted by him it extends to the disciplines of secular crafts, and from these disciplines or their distillations to the elements of theology and the gospel to which they pertain. We may hope that Barth would, after all, have recognized this affinity.

Thus despite Barth's misgivings, the way may be seen as open to a Barthian natural theology or, more precisely, a natural theology consistent with his principles. Our formulation goes beyond what either Barth or Brunner provided. In fact, it goes beyond what other theologians have had the resources to come up with, resulting in key issues of natural theology left unresolved and theology itself left in a degree of crisis, although it may not have been recognized as such. However, our formulation, provided it withstands scrutiny, could overcome this crisis, enabling theology to move forward again. In his 1934 essay, Brunner asserted, "It is the task of our theological generation to find the way back to a true *theologia naturalis* [natural theology]." We would have reservations about "the way back," having held that there has been no adequate natural theology to go back to—while still recognizing the need to take account of what has gone before. Our formulation indeed follows lines other than those that Brunner sketched out. But we would fully agree that our generation's task, for non-academic no less than academic theologians, is to devise a true natural theology. We have demonstrated, we hope, its possibility.

We should address some non-Barthian objections to our natural theology too. In our discussion, we have taken the "nature" in natural theology as referring primarily to the sphere of human activities, in particular professions and occupations, which we have subsumed under the heading of crafts. It might be objected that there are other spheres to which theology needs to be related, notably philosophy and the natural sciences, and that our treatment of the subject is, therefore, insufficient. Some might say that on this account it is not even a proper natural theology. However, two basic principles that we have advanced here, coming out of the Pentecost event as foundation for natural theology, can be seen as applicable to these spheres. The first principle is to take theology as our point of departure, as having priority in terms of being to any of these spheres, while at the same time constituting their *telos,* the end to which they finally point. The second is to regard philosophical concepts and the methods and findings of the natural sciences as capable of illuminating theology only when the Holy Spirit first has illuminated them. Only then can those spheres qualify as McGrath's *ancillae theologiae*, or handmaids of theology.

There is a further non-Barthian objection to address. In the attributions to the disciplines of the Foreign Service and other crafts that we have made, we might be regarded as uncritically affirming these crafts, and with them the world out of which they come. But this is not the case. First, as already noted, it is not the disciplines themselves but the distillations of them that we are looking to for the illumination of theology. And in the process of distillation their secularity has already undergone refinement. Further, their use in this way does not preclude theological judgment of the world. On the contrary, as clarified and deepened by their illumination theology will be the more empowered to stand over against the world. Ambrose, the great fourth century Bishop of Milan, likely owed part of his ability to require penance of the Emperor Theodosius for the massacre he had ordered in Thessalonica to the disciplines of his own prior career as a Roman civil servant.

The Fruits of our Barthian Natural Theology

Our formulation can thus be seen as a critical contribution to theology. No less importantly, it can be seen as providing the valid link which we have all along been seeking between theology on the one hand and the disciplines of the Foreign Service and other crafts—and thus the world—on the other. And this, we have said, makes possible the meeting of the two urgent needs described at the beginning of this Epilogue: that of the world for meaning as such and that of theology for the meaning afforded by contact with the world. For the world's potential to contribute to theology confers meaning on the world at the same time that contact with the world fructifies theology. To the extent that this is so, the main purpose of our undertaking will have been fulfilled.

On a lesser but still significant level, our formulation bears on the evident dividing issue in the church today, as alluded to in the Preface. This issue, dividing Anglicans and others too, is commonly regarded as relating to sexuality: to what extent should practicing non-heterosexuals be affirmed by the church? Underlying this issue, however, is one of biblical obedience:

should we conform the Scriptures to our experience or should our experience and the meaning we attach to it be conformed to them? Our answer to the first question derives largely from our answer to the second. Those who hold to conforming the Scriptures rather than being conformed by them may fear, not without some justification, that their conformity would result in the suppression of their experience and of their critical faculties too. But our approach calls for the employment of experience and critical faculties to the full—in elucidating rather than conforming the Scriptures. And on the premise that in scriptural obedience lies our peace and our joy, their employment in this elucidation can only be fruitful and unifying.

And in the light of the original Pentecost event, with which we have framed our enterprise, these possibilities entail the further possibility held out in the Prologue, namely that of a new Pentecost, wherein the gospel, having through the Holy Spirit illuminated the elements of human experience, is illumined by them in turn, so as to be newly empowered. There is, in fact, a historical precedent for such an outcome. The revival in Renaissance Italy of industry, commerce, and finance, all of which may be included under the heading of crafts, led to a cultural flowering. But this flowering did not stop with the arts, for which the period is famous. It extended also to the intellectual movement known as humanism, in which the writings of Cicero, Seneca, and others from ancient Rome were revived and studied and philological disciplines were developed to establish accurate versions of their texts. The philological disciplines, or rather distillations of them, spread from Italy to northern Europe, where as illuminated by the Holy Spirit they came to be applied to the Scriptural texts. As illuminated by them in turn, these texts turned out to have meanings markedly different from those generally accepted in the Middle Ages. And these rediscovered Scriptural meanings played a crucial role in the Reformation. Concretely, the good Greek text of the New Testament established by the humanist scholar Erasmus of Rotterdam in the early sixteenth century had a major impact on all the principal Reformers: Luther, Calvin, and Zwingli.

Becoming Oneself a Theologian
(or at least theologically literate)

If I have indeed shown that these potentials exist in the disciplines of the Foreign Service and other crafts, then the requirements for justifying the cost of my discovery and the reader's continuing interest, cited at this

Epilogue

Epilogue's beginning, will have been met. But the task is still not complete. Our formulation of natural theology is an outline rather than a completed structure. It needs the filling in to which scrutiny by theologians academic and non-academic can lead. Even more, the existence of similar potentials in the disciplines of crafts other than the Foreign Service, without which our formulation would have only local significance, is at this stage more a presumption than a proven conclusion. To establish it widely, and thus firmly, these potentials will need to be brought to light by those formed in the disciplines of these other crafts. Indeed, there may be further potentials in Foreign Service disciplines to be discerned and to be made known. To the persons formed in such disciplines, therefore, falls the responsibility that already in the Prologue I ascribed to them. This was the discernment and articulation of these potentials. Along with responsibility comes opportunity, in this case to participate in something so momentous as a new Pentecost. And to grasp this opportunity, and to be grasped by it, affords no possibility other than seeking to fulfil it with all one's "heart and soul and mind and strength."

For those so grasped, those to whom the Holy Spirit has given this vocation, the question arises of how to fulfil it, so as to make known the theological potential of their crafts. This question harks back to the question of whether there is "life after the Foreign Service," which my former colleagues in Paris raised with me as recounted at the beginning of the Prologue. There is indeed life—life more abundant than ever, though it does not come without cost. But I have no program to offer for its realization, nor do I believe that one exists. Essentially, each person called to it must work out his or her own answer "in fear and trembling." Perhaps, though, I can offer some guidance, to conclude this Epilogue.

In order to discern the links of craft disciplines with theology it is, of course, necessary to be formed in these disciplines. However, one needs to know theology; since the basis of theological knowledge is the Scriptures, one must become thoroughly versed in them, as by constant reading and rereading. Familiarity, though necessary, is not sufficient for understanding. A competence in biblical criticism and the insights of biblical scholars is also required. And as I have said, reading them in the original Greek and Hebrew gives them a special force and clarity. As for how to acquire a competence in biblical scholarship and, if at all possible, in biblical Greek and Hebrew, much of this can be done through one's own study. But for the acquisition of a thorough biblical knowledge, study in a community cannot be dispensed with. Theological seminaries afford such communities. As my experience shows, no small tribulations may be encountered in them (see chapter 3). But these may need to be braved anyway, trusting that the Lord will in the end set them aside.

Theology, however, did not spring forth full-blown from the Scriptures, like Minerva from the head of Zeus. Instead it was elaborated in the course of the church's history down through the centuries, as already described in the Prologue and in this Epilogue. And an understanding of this history is, for this reason, required. For theology cannot be separated from the church, in which it has developed and for the sake of which it exists. Moreover, the church is the necessary medium through which the links between theology and the world, which have been our concern, are actualized.

Theology itself needs to be comprehended: the thought of such figures as Augustine, Aquinas, Luther, Calvin, and Barth. Considerations similar to those applying to the acquisition of biblical knowledge apply here. Much can be done through one's own study. The many textbooks of Alister McGrath, outstanding in their lucidity and authority, can be enormously helpful here, as can the distinctive insights contained in the books of Stanley Hauerwas. But again, formation in a community is needed, whether a seminary or some other. As for what comprehension of all three of these fields—Scripture, church history, and theology as such—consists in, it is in arriving at the point not so much of mastering them as of being mastered by them, so that one no longer stands outside the Christian faith looking in, but instead stands inside looking out.

There are further considerations beyond these. I could not have accomplished what I have had I not placed myself under the tutelage of McGrath and Hauerwas, as I have already acknowledged. The question, then, arises of how to make similar connections. To be sure, special circumstances aided me in making mine, but no small daring was required. Without going to England, where I knew scarcely anybody, to work on my previous book, I would not have come in contact with McGrath, whom I had never heard of before. And confronting Hauerwas, to whom I had no introduction, in the Duke Divinity parking lot required a chutzpah of which I am capable only when desperate. If others will so dare, the Lord, who calls us to take risks in faith, may be trusted to reward them too. Actually, even eminent theologians, busy as they are, can be surprisingly responsive to those they perceive as genuinely interested in and comprehending of their work. Crucially, one needs to be a good listener.

Epilogue

Theological knowledge is a necessary but still not sufficient condition. One must not only learn theology but also do it. Otherwise one's knowledge cannot be effective, as with a computer program that has been downloaded but not installed. One needs also to have a project in which this knowledge is utilized. Along with fixing knowledge already acquired in one's mind, such a project will show where additional knowledge is needed, while enabling those one turns to for help to see its relevance. My book, *To Restore the Church,* over which I labored for so many years, well met these requirements. Other sorts of projects could meet them, too. Not any old project will do, though; it must concern something that one is keen about. Having such a project in mind may in fact be the best test of whether one is truly called to theology.

Most importantly, in the process of acquiring theological knowledge one must lay aside all pretensions to authority deriving from status in one's previous craft, however eminent this may have been, or from age either. It is necessary to be trusting rather than critical, as an apprentice is of a master, to become for a time like a child, counting one's previous formation as insignificant, albeit this may be difficult for former ambassadors and their equivalents in other crafts. Jesus spoke of the need to receive the kingdom of heaven as a child in order to enter it (Luke 18:17). Later, one can and should resume being critical, bringing one's craft formation and its disciplines fully to bear, but this only after establishing a theological framework. In this connection, I might note that all three of my main mentors, McGrath, Hauerwas, and Roy Wehrle in Saigon, were younger than I, McGrath by twenty-six years.

A final question is whether those called to learn theology are called also to exercise an ordained ministry, as I have. The answer could well be yes. Seeking ordination can facilitate access to seminaries and the training they afford. As ordained, one has special opportunities for linking theology and the world. To be sure, obtaining ordination can be arduous, as my experience abundantly testifies. After it is obtained, locating a suitable church position, even as a non-stipendiary (unpaid), may still be difficult. And once installed in such a position, one may find the church's other clergy, though sympathetic theologically, to be less than fully accepting. For those disciplined in a secular craft bring an asset lacked by those not so formed, or failing to recognize its potential if they are. And they may hesitate to acknowledge this asset.

Thus the path for those called to actualize the contribution of craft disciplines to theology and the church may be rocky despite my pioneering of it. But those so called and failing to respond will not only be evading their responsibility. They will also be foregoing a chance to participate in so cardinal an event as a new Pentecost. Moreover, they will have left the deeper significances of their craft disciplines unfathomed.

ANNEX

The Book Recast as Sermon: Pentecost as Imperative
(Acts 2:1–47)

All Saints' Church | Chevy Chase, Maryland | Pentecost, 2014

PENTECOST, ALONG WITH CHRISTMAS and Easter, is one of the great festivals of the Christian year. But it is not really about speaking in tongues as we may have supposed. Instead, it is about the church's Big Bang, the point, however small, from which it spread throughout the ancient world with amazing rapidity. In this spread the Holy Spirit, having descended on the disciples as they met together at Pentecost, is to be seen as having played the crucial role. It is vital that we understand how this is so—for we are called to a new Pentecost today.

These three assertions—about Pentecost as the point from which the church so rapidly spread, about the crucial role of the Holy Spirit in its spread, about the imperative that this role imposes on us—mean that the Pentecost event, far from being static, is supremely dynamic. (They are also the points of my three-point sermon.) And they depend on a special interpretation of the Pentecost event, one that came to me while I was still at seminary—I graduated fifty years ago last month. They depend also on the book, *Theology and the Disciplines of the Foreign Service*, which I am now completing; this particular interpretation of Pentecost turned out to constitute the book's indispensable hinge. I will speak about the book later but first about how this interpretation came to me and what it was.

I was the seminarian at St. Margaret's Church, off Connecticut up from DuPont Circle. On Pentecost Sunday, I was designated to read the Epistle as it was then called, the account in Acts 2 of the descent of the Holy Spirit on the gathered disciples, impelling them to proclaim the wonderful works God—the gospel—to the crowd of bystanders whom they had attracted. I was told of my designation only a couple of minutes before the service began. Thus I had no time to work out the pronunciation of the long list of the origins of these bystanders: Phrygia, Pamphylia, Cappadocia, and the like. I could then see only two options. One was to slur over the origins, hoping to obscure my ineptitude. The other was to pronounce them boldly, as if I knew what I was talking about. I chose the latter. To my surprise, afterwards a young woman in the congregation came up to me saying how impressive the list had sounded as I read it.

This got me to thinking. Although this list may seem random to us, it would not have to the ancients, swinging as it does around the eastern end of the Mediterranean and then proceeding west as far as Rome. It likely represented the places that the gospel had got to by the time Acts was written down, probably in the latter part of the first century, perhaps 80 AD. There is, in fact, support for this interpretation in the Acts passage. Its list includes no places in Greece or of Greek speech like Alexandria in Egypt. There would have been nothing remarkable about Greek speakers hearing the gospel in Greek, the language in which it was generally proclaimed, as instanced by the New Testament being written in Greek.

It is not just on where the church had got to by then but also on how it was received there that this interpretation casts light. The model is already in Acts 2; I invite you to look at the text. This chapter says that these diverse bystanders heard the disciples' Spirit-inspired proclamation in their native languages, literally "in which we were born." This conveys that they heard it in terms of what was most intimate for them, not just their languages but their traditions and occupations, perhaps especially their occupations since these took up so much of their time. We may speak of these elements as their cognitive elements, those in terms of which they thought.

Following from this, Peter, himself impelled by the Holy Spirit, addresses them, connecting the disciples' speech that they have just heard with the death and resurrection of Jesus. Drawing on the Day of the Lord as spoken of by the Prophet Joel, he confronts them with their responsibility, albeit only indirect, for Jesus' death. He sets out how starkly what they have done to Jesus contrasts with God's raising him from the dead. And they are "cut to the heart." That is to say, they are convicted and converted by what Peter has told them. Seeing this, Peter assures them of their forgiveness in Jesus, calling on them to be baptized in his name. In large numbers, they answer his call. But this is not all. Having answered it, they become themselves the agents of the church's spread, proclaiming the gospel to those around them. To be sure, this is not said explicitly. But it is implicit in the chapter's final verse. It tells us, "the Lord added to their number day by day." The proclamation by Peter and the other disciples, important as it was, could have been no more than part of what took place.

What was going on here and what did it have to do with the spread of the early church? These are crucial questions, and the answers are crucial. The Holy Spirit, acting through Peter's pronouncement to the bystanders, transformed them, but it also transformed their languages, traditions, and occupations, the elements in terms of which they conceived of things. As touched by the Spirit these elements, their cognitive elements, became lenses through which they saw their lives in a new way, saw them as no longer random or incoherent but instead as falling into patterns. The pattern they particularly saw here consisted of their sin, their need for redemption, and the possibility of it in Jesus. In connection with this, we may think of iron filings lying randomly on a sheet of paper but then standing up and positioning themselves around the poles of a magnet held beneath them.

Viewed from a slightly different angle, these elements of daily life were not just illuminated by the gospel; they illuminated it in turn. In so doing, they enabled the bystanders to see still further implications of the gospel for their lives. The bystanders, then, were equipped proclaim the gospel, and to do so with power. Thus along with the disciples they too became agents of the church's rapid spread. To be sure, St. Paul and probably others as well went on extensive missionary journeys. But for the most part, evidently, the church spread through its ordinary members as they came in contact with those around them. Joel, in the passage that Peter referred to in addressing the bystanders, spoke not just of the Day of the Lord. He spoke also of "your sons and daughters" prophesying in that Day. The proclamation which following Pentecost the converted bystanders went on to make fulfils Joel's prophesy.

So much for what is said to have gone on in Jerusalem. What about the reception of the gospel later on, by peoples in places such as those the

Acts passage lists? The passage provides a model for it, as I have said. As the gospel was proclaimed to these peoples, they too would have heard it in terms of their own languages, traditions, and occupations. As viewed through these lenses their lives took on a coherence they had not had before, allowing their redemption from their sins. And the gospel itself became luminous for them, so that they became both able and impelled to proclaim it in their turn. It is worth noting that none of the languages native to these places has survived; in the face of the universalizing Greek and Latin of the day, eventually they all gave way. But the pressures they were already being subjected to would have made hearing the gospel in them the more precious to those who still spoke them.

How, though, does what happened in the early church relate to us moderns? Unless the Holy Spirit can use our cognitive elements of language, tradition, and occupation to illumine the gospel and to spread of the church, what he did on and following the Day of Pentecost is of only limited interest. But he can so use our cognitive elements; this is the essential point of my nearly completed book. I will here focus on how our occupations and their disciplines can be available for his use.

As you may know, I had a career in the Foreign Service, a career demanding a particularly intense commitment. And its disciplines became an important part of my cognitive apparatus—indeed, the main part. My book is basically about how in the course of my Foreign Service career I discovered links between these disciplines and theology. These links illumined theology and thus the gospel for me, clarifying and deepening its meaning. In fact, they became my main channel into its meaning. Here is one example:

The central function of the Foreign Service is to report back to Washington what is going on in other countries. Among the indications of what is going on are the pronouncements of public figures, governmental and otherwise. In the Foreign Service, you learn never to take these pronouncements at face value. This is not to say that they are meaningless; indeed, they can be highly meaningful. But you need to probe beneath the surface, to ascertain their underlying motivations, before this meaning becomes apparent. On arriving at seminary, I was introduced to modern biblical criticism. One of its conclusions is that accounts of Jesus' ministry in the Gospels are not to be taken as those of eyewitnesses. Instead, they are seen as having circulated orally in the communities of faith for some decades before being written down. In this way, they came to reflect the meaning

The Book Recast as Sermon: Pentecost as Imperative

that they had for these communities, in the face of the severe difficulties with which they were confronted.

Immediately, I recognized the affinity between the approach of biblical criticism and the critical approach I had developed in the Foreign Service. I would not have been open to it, however, had I not already been touched by the Holy Spirit and so converted. And this recognition led me to a whole new appreciation of the gospel accounts. For in seeing what they meant to the communities that preserved them, how they enabled these communities to stand in the face of persecution and other trials to which they were subjected, I could see with a new clarity what they meant for us today. I was impelled to communicate my new appreciation to others; in fact, to do so became my special vocation, as led by the Holy Spirit.

The Foreign Service is not the only profession or occupation to have its disciplines; one thinks here of law or medicine, but others, such as bricklaying, have them, too. This is the case even with parenting, perhaps especially with parenting. When touched by the Holy Spirit, the practitioners of these professions and occupations become able to recognize the links of these disciplines with theology and the gospel. They can see also how these links cast light on the gospel, not only enhancing their own understanding of it but also equipping and compelling them to proclaim it.

So far, abilities such as these have existed mainly as potentials. Their existence may not have dawned on those whom professional and occupational disciplines have formed, even after the Holy Spirit has brought about their conversion. But the interpretation of Pentecost adduced here, as elaborated in my book, as summarized in this sermon, constitutes a summons to their recognition, an imperative to realize their potentials. Paul at the Areopagus tells the Athenians that "the times of ignorance God overlooked, but now he commands all people everywhere to repent" (Acts 17). It is by virtue of this summons, then, that those hearing it and failing to answer will be without excuse. But if they do answer this summons, do respond to this imperative, they will find themselves contributing decisively to the spread of the church in our time. Indeed, they will be among those opening the way to a new Pentecost, the ultimate dynamic of the church.

May this dynamic, the power of the Holy Spirit manifested at the first Pentecost, come upon us all.

The Rev. Theodore L. Lewis

www.ingramcontent.com/pod-product-compliance
Lightning Source LLC
Chambersburg PA
CBHW071454150426
43191CB00008B/1345